WHAT ROLE DO I PLAY?

Learning to Control and Change Your Roles in Life

WHAT ROLE DO I PLAY?

Learning to Control and Change Your Roles in Life

MIKE SIVER MAC, CDVC, BCBC
& APRIL SIVER MED

PUBLISHED BY FIDELI PUBLISHING, INC.

ISBN: 978-1-60414-984-5

MIKE SIVER
Business Center
49770 East Dr.
Decatur, MI 49045

Contact the author at: mgsiver@gmail.com

For more information, visit:
www.MikeSiver.com

Cover Illustration by Paisley Hansen

Table of Contents

Preface ....*ix*

Introduction ....*xi*

CHAPTER 1   Your Role as You....................................... 1

CHAPTER 2   The Sponge.. 3

CHAPTER 3   Listen to the Wind 8

CHAPTER 4   A Better Future 11

CHAPTER 5   Thanks to Our Protectors................... 14

CHAPTER 6   Your Role is a River 17

CHAPTER 7   The Lesson... 19

CHAPTER 8   Making Friends 21

CHAPTER 9   Keeping Friends.................................... 24

CHAPTER 10   Pride... 27

CHAPTER 11   Listen and Learn.................................. 29

CHAPTER 12   Look, Listen, Act 31

CHAPTER 13   Change Your Role 33

CHAPTER 14   Win Well, Lose Well.............................. 35

CHAPTER 15   The Little Boy and the Old Man.......... 38

CHAPTER 16   Love Your Role 41

CHAPTER 17   Time Management 43

CHAPTER 18   Good When Convenient 47

CHAPTER 19   Keeping Your Word 51

CHAPTER 20   Better Than Yesterday 54

CHAPTER 21   Make Your Role Work for You 57

CHAPTER 22   Encourage Innovation 59

CHAPTER 23   Perception 61

CHAPTER 24   Helping Hand 64

CHAPTER 25   Being Liked 67

CHAPTER 26   Play Your Role Like a Rock 70

CHAPTER 27   Follower or Leader 72

CHAPTER 28   Cool Off 75

CHAPTER 29   Happiness 77

CHAPTER 30   Teach Our Children 80

CHAPTER 31   Teach Children About Roles 84

CHAPTER 32   Is it Working? 86

CHAPTER 33   Patient or Enabling 89

CHAPTER 34   Message or Messenger 92

CHAPTER 35   How to Become a Bully 95

CHAPTER 36   The Victim Role.. 98

CHAPTER 37   Parent as a Role Model 100

CHAPTER 38   Leader as a Role Model 103

CHAPTER 39   Hatred.. 105

CHAPTER 40   Building Bridges... 108

CHAPTER 41   Don't Burn Bridges 111

CHAPTER 42   How Far You Go.. 114

CHAPTER 43   Who or What is Right or Wrong? 116

CHAPTER 44   Play Your Role Well..................................... 119

CHAPTER 45   Be Successful... 122

CHAPTER 46   Forced to Agree 125

CHAPTER 47   Protect Our Freedom.................................. 128

CHAPTER 48   Don't Be Ashamed 130

CHAPTER 49   Two Ears, One Mouth 132

CHAPTER 50   Guilty By Accusation 135

CHAPTER 51   Your Future Roles.. 138

CHAPTER 52   Your Name 140

              About the Authors 145

Preface

While re-writing this book, I asked Kirk Dusek (my nephew) to read it and give me his opinion. When he finished reading, one of the things he informed me was missing was any reference to God.

While we both know not everyone believes in God, he and I both are aware that without God acting in our own lives we more than likely would not be here to write this stuff.

Kirk has first-hand experience with what's discussed in this book. His life was on the wrong track for a number of years. Even with everything he had been through and everything he knew, he realized that nothing was working for him.

He says nothing changed for him until he was introduced to God. Soon after that, he found a simple and solid way to redirect his life and future.

After talking with Kirk, I asked him if he would like to collaborate on this book and add things he'd learned as well as things that had worked for him. He happily agreed and we now have a book gives readers a practical way to improve their life skills, plus the added benefit of scripture to suit each situation.

Introduction

"What role do I play?" is a question we could all ben-efit from asking ourselves about our daily lives. What role we play and how we play that role can make the difference between success and failure. While at times we can't change the role we are playing, we do have control over how we are playing that role.

I can play the role of adult daughter in a way that makes my parents feel loved and safe and secure, or I can play the same role in a way that makes them feel frightened and alone.

I can change my employee role from one of the untrustworthy and ineffective employee to that of dependable and productive, and I can do it just by paying attention to my actions.

The purpose of this book is to offer insight and tools that will allow individuals to empower themselves to look at the roles we are playing and evaluate how we are playing those roles, and helping us make changes as we believe we need to.

This is a concept most of us do not think about, and once we begin to consider it in our own lives, we realize how much power we have and how much more enjoyable our lives can be.

If we had to put this book into a category, it would be *SelfHelp*. The book is designed to be used by individuals, families, groups, or classes. We tried to write it in a way that would be effective in any of these situations. The content is divided into 52 weeks or chapters, with the intent that it be used as a weekly guide for one year.

We believe this book lends itself to an ongoing study that can help as an individual or a group continues a focus on self-improvement. The authors are Christian, so we used our personal spiritual guide, the Christian Bible (NIV), to design a supplement that includes 52 passages of scripture as an addendum to each week. These are included throughout the book at the end of each chapter as a proven option for change for those struggling. We encourage others to create a similar supplement to provide support for discussion based on their religion or ideas.

CHAPTER 1

Your Role as You

Wherever you are in life; you can start today to take charge of your role as a human being. You can decide what your role of a family member will be. You may be a great family member; the one who holds everything together and who can always be counted on, or you may be the one who always counts on the others. No matter where you are now, you can change what you don't like and improve on the areas you do like. It's all about how you play the role.

You play many roles in life, but none as important as the role of you. You are the only you, and no one can tell you how to play the role of you because no one else knows how. Play it well!

The same thing holds true in your role as an employee, student, neighbor, committee member, friend, etc. Each day you play many roles throughout the day, and how you play them is determined by you. How you play them also builds the role of you as perceived by the rest of your world. After you play the role of grumpy coworker long enough, it will stay with you and will become the expectation of others when they see you.

It is up to you to decide if you are ready to make some changes to the role of you. This can only be done with some effort and flexibility, and hopefully a sense of humor. If you are going to build a new and better role of you, why not make it one you enjoy playing, and that others enjoy being around.

Above all else, guard your heart, for everything you do flows from it.

Scripture for Thought

Whoever pursues righteousness and love finds life, prosperity and honor.

Proverbs 21:21

Add a scripture or quote of your own that will help you relate to this week's topic.

_____

_____

_____

CHAPTER 2

The Sponge

The article below is included in this book because it fits, and it is a foundational piece that helps each of us to put our own personal life situation into perspective. As you read it, please keep in mind what role you are playing at this point in time, how you are playing that role, and if you would like to change how you are playing it.

If a child is given love, he becomes loving ... If he's helped when he needs help, he becomes helpful. And if he has been truly valued at home ... he grows up secure enough to look beyond himself to the welfare of others.

— Dr. Joyce Brothers

The Sponge
Words to live by, from a father to his children

When a baby is born, he is like a new sponge, clean and empty. There is neither love nor hate within him.

That newborn baby, just like a new sponge, will absorb whatever atmosphere he is placed in at the time. If the atmosphere is one that includes love, support, kindness, honesty, fair play, ethical thinking, and acceptance of others, then this is what will be absorbed.

If the atmosphere is full of hate, distrust, lying, drugs, alcohol, bigotry, racism, and an *all for ME attitude*; then that will be absorbed.

Whatever atmosphere you grow up in, you, like the sponge, will keep absorbing until you are full. Then, whatever you are full of will start to flow back out.

If that is love, kindness, honesty, fair play, ethical thinking and acceptance of others, then that is what you will give back to those around you in your family and community.

If you fill up on hate, distrust, lying, drugs or alcohol, bigotry, and racism, then that is what you will give back to your family and community.

Unlike the sponge, as you get older, you have a choice of what you want to absorb. If you are in an unhealthy family or community, it may be very hard to stop absorbing the bad and make a change, because you know that to do so will make you different. You know that when you are different from your family or community, you will have to be very strong. The important thing to learn here is that every time you are strong, and you make your own decision, you gain power.

> *"The greatest power we have as a human*
> *is the ability to make a choice."*

Sometimes you start to wonder, "What role am I playing in my life?' If you do not like what you discover, and you decide to change, you could need some help.

This help could be compared to wringing out the sponge. When the sponge is put in a clean bowl of water, it will only *start* to become clean. It usually takes a few good rinses to completely clean a sponge. In the same way, it may take you several efforts and possibly a long time to change from an unhealthy person to a healthy person. The help you need may come in many forms. It could be moving out of an unhealthy atmosphere, maybe going to jail, going to a rehabilitation or behavior program, participating in individual or family counseling, or finding religion.

As we all know, when we clean a dirty sponge in a bowl of water, the first bowl of clean water will become dirty and may have to be changed several times before the sponge is clean enough, and the water is coming out of it clear. Like the sponge, depending on how long and how unhealthy the atmosphere was you might have to make several attempts to change your behavior or become clean.

Without realizing what you are doing, you will often try to make the new environment like the one you left, because that is your comfort zone, and up until now, that was all you knew.

Good or bad, the environment you were brought up in is your comfort zone. You may not like the environment, but at least you know what is going to happen in almost every situation.

Most of us want our environment to be one we are comfortable in, and we hope it is good, but good or bad we want to know what is going to happen next. The new environment may be very uncomfortable because you never know what is going to happen. This is where the demand for consistent support from others is the strongest.

Changing the environment is not enough, there must also be love and understanding combined with a lot of education about how to make those changes.

The education isn't just for you, but may also have to involve your family and community. Everyone involved with you must have the same education to be able to provide you with the support you need. This education, mixed with love and care, will help you live through this, and with time be able to break the mold. You can then take on the responsibility of a person who will one day be proud of "What role you are playing."

Scripture for Thought

The Lord is with you when you are with him. If you seek him, he will be found by you, but if you forsake him, he will forsake you.

2 Chronicles 15:2

From now on, brothers and sisters, if anything is excellent and if anything, is admirable, focus your thoughts on these things: all that is true, all that is holy, all that is just, all that is pure, all that is lovely, and all that is worthy of praise, think on these things.

Philippians 4:8

Add a scripture or quote of your own that will help you relate to this week's topic.

_____

_____

_____

CHAPTER 3

Listen to the Wind

The winds brings all the sounds of our lives to us if we just listen. When we first step outside, we hear our thoughts. Then as we stand still and start to listen, those thoughts will be interrupted by some nearby sounds, like a car's motor, or a horn honking. If you continue to listen, you will begin to hear the sound of the leaves rustling in the treetop, and maybe the flap of the wings of a bird as he flys by. Sometimes, if the wind is very

When was the last time you stopped and listened to the wind? Listening to the wind demands you give yourself permission to take 10 minutes out of your life and just listen to the sounds around you. You may actually hear something new and exciting.

— Bill Orr

strong; you can hear it whistle as it blows. But you hear none of this if you don't stop and listen.

This is where you ask yourself, what role am I playing in my limited ability to hear my world? Am I the one keeping myself too busy to stop and listen?

Before you can hear your world, you must give yourself permission to take some personal, private time and stop worrying for a few minutes each day. By doing this, you may discover something new and exciting about yourself, those around you, or your environment.

The longer you practice listening to your world, the more you will be able to hear.

If you sit long enough, you may be able to tune everything out and just hear peace.

Scripture for Thought;

The earth is the Lord's, and everything in it, the world, and all who live in it.

Psalm 24:1

...[A]nd a cloud overshadowed them, and a voice came out of the cloud, This is my beloved Son; listen to him.

Mark 9:7

Making your ear attentive to wisdom and inclining your heart to understanding.

Proverbs 2:2

Add a scripture or quote of your own that will help you relate to this week's topic.

_____

_____

_____

CHAPTER 4

A Better Future

It's a shame that we have to wait until we get older to recognize that time is a great teacher. If we look back on our life from today, we will see the things in our past that really bothered us at the time. Some of those things will seem like perfect examples

You make your future better only when you become better. You become better when you change the way you play your life roles. You change how you play your roles when you take the time to look at how you are playing those roles now. You improve your life now when you decide how you want to play your life roles, and you do what it takes to make that happen. You have a better future because you changed today.

of *making a mountain out of a molehill*. They seemed very important at the time, yet today we can see that they were almost insignificant in the big picture of our lives.

What we need to do is look back at how we were playing our role in the situation, and figure out how we could have done it differently. Now we remember that as we look at situations in our lives today, and evaluate how we are playing our role there. Are we still making a mountain out of a molehill? If so, how can we change what we are doing to make our life easier?

We have control of how we play our roles in every situation we are in, and IF we use our experience from the past, we will make our future so much better.

Test

Take some time, get a piece of paper and make three columns. In the first column, write down all the valuable lessons, both positive and negative, that you learned over the last 12 months. Please consider that many of the things you will want to improve on, some you will never do again, and some you can't wait to do again. Everything on your list has value. *even the negitive ones*

Next, in the second column write down how you played your role in the situation. Were you passive or aggressive, mean or nice, lazy or energetic, etc., etc.? There is no one answer for any of this.

Last, in the third column, write down how you wish you would have played your role. What could you have done differently that would have changed a bad situation into a good thing, or at least into a bad thing with less harm done?

The lessons are what you carry with you into the future. As you look at them, try to make this activity a lesson. From now on, as you encounter a situation, look at how you are playing your role in it, and how you could change your behavior to end up with the best possible results. This is how you will create a better future. *what you could do different*

and called learning from your mistakes

Valuable Lessons	My Role	What I Should've Done

Scripture for Thought

Blessed is the one who perseveres under trial because, having stood the test, that person will receive the crown of life that the Lord has promised to those who love him.

James 1:12

Add a scripture or quote of your own that will help you relate to this week's topic.

_____

_____

_____

one day a fire started in a shop a couple doors from my shop.

Thanks to Our Protectors

As a merchant/shop owner in Decatur, MI the need for a fire department to respond urgently and efficiently was never more obvious to me ~~than on that day~~.

The willingness of these firefighters to put themselves in danger for our safety, and the protection of our property, became clear that day, and I gained a new appreciation for all of our public service officers.

My ~~Our~~ gratitude for their willingness to put themselves in danger for our safety cannot be expressed enough.

I want to give personal thanks to the Decatur/ Hamilton Fire Department for their fast and efficient action on February 5, 2008.

—Mike Siver

Mamaia Kiitos Juspaxa Maake Ua Tsaug Rau Koj Mochchaldeeram Terma Kasih Multumesc Merci
Kia Ora *Grazie* Obrigado Asante Vinaka
Matondo Dank Je **THANK** Merci
Nirringnuzzjak Obrigado **YOU** Multumesc Spasib
Mochchaldeeram Spasib Kiitos
Nirringnuzzjak Multumesc
Matur Nuwun Salamat Arigato Obrigado Welalin
Kiitos Chokrane Grade

the thanks is for risking their lives, and doing your job normally doesn't put you or your co-workers life at risk

A simple thanks seems so inadequate — so I say it again:

THANKS!

This is a reminder that in the United States we are very fortunate to have strong public service organizations — the local fire and police departments. In many instances, these positions are volunteer, or often very low paying jobs.

It is time to ask yourself, what role do you play in providing public safety to your family and community? What would happen to your community if every public service officer quit their job tomorrow?

Every American adult holds some of the responsibility to ensure that our communities are safe.

Many times we take the services that these Public Safety Officers provide for granted. It is a common thing to hear someone say in anger, "Where are those policemen?" Or, "Why did it take the fire department so long to get to that burning house?"

These comments are made as though it is the fault of the fire department that someone's home caught fire [burned down] when in reality it is often the fault of the homeowners themselves. [the building cought fire in the first place]

Other comments commonly heard include: "It's their job, and they get paid to do it, so why should I give them extra thanks. No one gives me extra thanks for doing my job." "If they don't want to do the job, they can just quit. They are the ones who signed up for it. No one makes them do it."

While there may be some pieces of truth to these statements, they are not important when it comes to our safety, and they need to stop. If this is the role you decide to play regarding our public safety officers, you should reconsider. Why not reevaluate

15

your role in your safety, and start to make attempts to show your appreciation to the brave men and women who protect us every day.

Take the $10 you were going to spend on that movie, and instead, buy a movie pass and give it to the next police officer or firefighter you see. Or when your school has a fundraiser, buy that box of chocolates but have them deliver it to the fire station or police station instead of you.

Take on a new role, that of a giver of gratitude.

Scripter for Thought

His master replied, 'Well done, good and faithful servant! You have been faithful with a few things; I will put you in charge of many things. Come and share your master's happiness!'

Matthew 25:21

Greater love hath no man than this, that a man lay down his life for his friends.

John 15:13

blessed are the peacemakers; for they shall be called the children of God.

Matthew 5:9

Add a scripture or quote of your own that will help you relate to this week's topic.

CHAPTER 6

Your Role is a River

E ach day many of us play roles similar to the roles we played the day before. Why is it that some days are easy and very enjoyable, and some are so difficult we can barely get through them? It may be that we played the role different today, but it may also be that there were outside factors involved, over which we had no control.

When this happens, it might help to picture your role as a river. If you have never had the opportunity to watch a river flow, try to find one, or at least watch one on the internet. The thing about a river is that it doesn't let anything stop its flow, or do

No man ever steps in the same river twice, for it's not the same river and he's not the same man.

— Heraclitus

17

any more than slightly change its course. No matter how big the obstacle is that is blocking it, the water will still find a way to flow.

A good way to learn about the concept of a river is to ride down one in some type of boat. This provides a first-hand view of the river going over and around rocks and branches and making natural curves where the terrain requires it. This experience makes it easy to understand the role of the river. It remains fluid and flexible and moves around whatever is in its way, yet it always comes back to itself.

If you can learn to play all your life roles this way you may find your feeling of accomplishment increase, and your frustration level decrease. Work with what's in front of you and try to make accommodations that may be needed to get past whatever is in your way, yet do not give up the control of your role and how you play it.

Scripture for Thought

But let justice roll on like a river, righteousness like a never-failing stream!

Amos 5:24

Add a scripture or quote of your own that will help you relate to this week's topic.

_____

_____

_____

CHAPTER 7

The Lesson

"The greatest lesson in life is to know that
even fools are right sometimes"

— Winston Churchill

In the United States, as we play our role as a member of our community, it is important to play it in a non-judgmental way with an open mind. People are not always as they first appear to be.

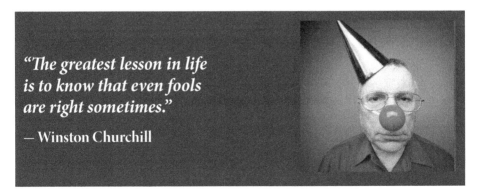

"The greatest lesson in life is to know that even fools are right sometimes."
— Winston Churchill

Whether we are in our work environment, our family home, our neighborhood meeting, or any other place where we play a community role, we will do well to remember that no one is always right, and no one is good or bad at everything. The person who can't seem to ever keep the budget straight may be able to play the piano like a professional. We all need to keep an open mind about everyone else as we hope they do about us.

You will play very different roles in different communities in your life. Make sure you play each one to the best of your ability. Also, make sure that you have the same expectations for others in your life as you want them to have for you. Keep your expectations high for everyone, and for your ability as a group to work together using each person's talents and skills for the best results for the community as a whole.

Scripture for Thought

The second is this: 'Love your neighbor as yourself.' There is no commandment greater than these.

Mark 12:31

Add a scripture or quote of your own that will help you relate to this week's topic.

_____

_____

_____

CHAPTER 8

Making Friends

Friends are important. In all cultures, at all age groups, we need friends. Friends come into our lives for various reasons, and much of the time we have the power to influence that, for better or for worse, and it is up to us how we use that power.

The question here is, what role do you play in building new friendships? Do you take an interest in someone, and let them

You can make more friends in two months by becoming interested in other people, than you can in two years by trying to get other people interested in you.

know that you have something in common, and you would like to hear what they have to say about it.

Or instead, do you take the role of impressing the potential new friend, and you try to get them to notice some specific thing about you in the hopes that they will find you interesting.

This is an easy thing to do an experiment with. First, play the role of an insecure person, who wears the latest fashion or hairdo, trying to get others to notice you. You will probably be noticed, but will not likely have any gestures of friendship put forward.

Now, play the role of friend, to someone you don't know well yet.

Watch for some action or activity that person is involved in. Walk up to them, and ask them about it, showing an interest in it, and in what they are saying. It is very likely that they will return the interest, and will be glad to carry on a personal conversation with you, which is often what leads to friendship.

It is the way you play your role as a future friend that makes the difference, not what you are wearing.

How you choose to play the friendship role will have a lifelong impact on your happiness.

Scripture for Thought

⁹Two are better than one, because they have a good return for their work, 10 If one falls down his friend can help him up. But pity the man who falls and has no one to help him up.

Ecclesiastes 4: 9-10

Do not be misled: "Bad company corrupts good character."

1 Corinthians 15:33

Add a scripture or quote of your own that will help you relate to this week's topic.

_____

_____

_____

CHAPTER 9

Keeping Friends

Friendships are important to most people. Friendships must be treated carefully if we want them to last a lifetime, and who doesn't want that. There is nothing so precious when you are entering your golden years than a visit with a close life-long friend. You can sit and talk for hours, telling stories and just remembering your shared experiences. This does not happen by accident. It takes work.

The reason dogs have so many friends is that they wag their tails instead of their tongues. We lose more friends by running our mouth than by any other action we do. If we could engage our brain before we engaged our mouth things would be so much better for us.

No matter what your age is, you should stop now and ask yourself, what role am I playing in my friendships? Am I doing what I can to maintain the relationship, or am I taking it for granted and ignoring it, and putting it in danger by making careless, negative comments to the friend, or worse yet, to others about the friend. Very few friendships can withstand the damage caused by gossip and rumors. Your role as a friend is to prevent the gossip, not to participate in it.

The role of a friend is one of the most important roles you will play in your life. It is where you gain many of your fondest memories. It doesn't matter if the friend is a childhood best friend, who stood by your side through many of your biggest life events; or if it is a casual friend from work, who you enjoy talking with, and you know you can count on in times of need at work. How you play that role has a lot to do with the day to day quality of your life. Those who play the role of a friend with selfishness and indifference will go through life much more alone than those who play the friend role with care and respect. If you would like to have a friend by your side when you are in a bad place in life, you have to make sure that being by your side is a comfortable and safe place for your friend to be.

Play this role with great care.

Scripture for Thought

Finally, brothers and sisters, rejoice! Strive for full restoration, encourage one another, be of one mind, live in peace. And the God of love and peace will be with you.

2 Corinthians 13:11

For if they fall, one will lift up his fellow. But woe to him who is alone when he falls and has not another to lift him up!

Ecclesiastes 4:10

Iron sharpens iron, and one man sharpens another. John 15:13 Greater love has no one than this, that someone lay down his life for his friends.

Proverbs 27:17

Add a scripture or quote of your own that will help you relate to this week's topic.

_____

_____

_____

CHAPTER 10

Pride

P lay your roles with pride. Whether it is your role as employee, spouse, parent, friend, or any other role, be proud of it and how you play it.

As Thomas Jefferson said in the quote below, no matter what you are doing, do it as if all the world were watching. If you keep this attitude with all the roles you play, you will always do your best.

Start with the small example of keeping your house clean. If you are not expecting any company, you will keep things reason-

"Whenever you do a thing, act as if all the world were watching."

— Thomas Jefferson

able, but you won't put yourself out to make things look great for the family who lives there.

Now you get a call, and your mother-in-law is coming by for a visit. Suddenly, you see that the house is a little messy, and you take some time to straighten things up before she arrives.

Oh, no! Now your mother-in-law calls and says she is bringing the mayor of your city with her to visit. All of a sudden you can see every little cobweb in the corner, and you rush around to get your home to the standard you think is expected.

If you had always played your homemaker role at the level you thought was expected, you would not be rushing around at the last minute to meet your standards.

Whatever roles you are playing, decide for yourself what your personal expectations are for each of these roles, and don't waiver from them. If you always strive to be your best, that is what you will be.

Scripture for Thought

A person may think their own ways are right, but the Lord weighs the heart.

Proverbs 21:2

Add a scripture or quote of your own that will help you relate to this week's topic.

_____

_____

_____

CHAPTER 11

Listen and Learn

Τhe old saying was and still is: "Don't make the same mistake I did." We make mistakes when we are children, even when we listen because sometimes we don't understand what we are told to do. We listen, but we don't learn.

Then, we make mistakes as teens because we don't listen — we think we know better. We don't listen, so we don't learn.

It's not until several years into adulthood that we start to understand another old saying… My parents got smarter as I got

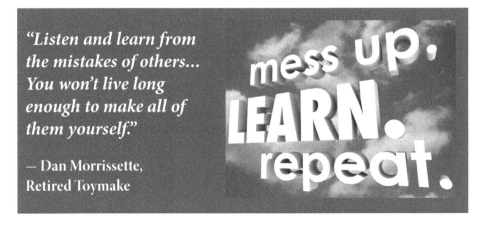

"Listen and learn from the mistakes of others... You won't live long enough to make all of them yourself."

— Dan Morrissette,
Retired Toymake

older. That is when we start to listen, not only to our parents but also to everyone else. We listen, and we learn.

It's at this point in our life when most of us start to listen and learn. We pay attention and listen when others tell us we shouldn't do something because it would be a mistake, or that it might be better if we try it another way.

There could be any number of things others are willing to share with us that they have learned from their own mistakes and the mistakes others made before them.

If we are smart we will, as Mr. Morrissette so amiably says,

"Listen and learn."

Scripture for Thought

Know this, my beloved brothers; let every person be quick to hear, slow to speak, slow to anger.

James 1:19

Making your ear attentive to wisdom and inclining your heart to understanding.

Proverbs 2:2

If one gives an answer before this hears, it is his folly and shame.

Proverbs 18:13

Add a scripture or quote of your own that will help you relate to this week's topic.

_____

_____

CHAPTER 12

Look, Listen, Act

M ost of us see and hear what is going on around us. Our perception of our world is pretty clear when we want it to be. If you have been around children much, you know they have an excellent ability to hear what is said when it is about ice cream but will insist that they never heard a word about cleaning their room. This is true for everyone in all stages of life — we often have selective vision and hearing. Often we choose to play the role of the observer in our lives, rather than the role of participant.

> *Do you look through open eyes, and still not see?*
> *Do you listen to what is said, but still not hear?*
> *Do you find a way to see the whole picture*
> *and hear the whole story?*
> *OR*
> *Do you only see or hear what you want to?*
> *What role do you play in being a person of honesty and*
> *integrity when it comes to taking in and acting on what is*
> *going on around you?*

Observing the things going on around you is not the problem, but doing nothing when you see something that requires attention is. You might think, *No one knows I saw it, so I don't have to do anything about it.*

Selective hearing — only hearing what you want to — can also be a problem. You could be receiving sound advice from caring people, but choose not to hear it. On the other hand, if someone tells us "juicy" gossip, we're all ears and ready to pass along what we heard to others.

We should participate in our lives, and pay attention to what is being said. If we hear someone spreading lies and rumors, we should take action and tell them to stop. You know right from wrong, so be sure your actions reflect this.

You should actively play the role of a person of honesty and integrity who takes responsibility for your world even when it isn't convenient. This is a role that is always within your power.

Scripture for Thought

The one who gets wisdom loves life; the one who cherishes understanding will soon prosper.

Proverbs 19:8

For the righteous falls seven times and rises again, but the wicked stumble in times of calamity.

Proverbs 24:16

I can do all things through him who strengthens me.

Philippians 4:13

CHAPTER 13

Change Your Role

I f you don't like the role you are playing, change it. It's as simple as that. You have the power to control your behavior, and thus the roles you play and the way you play them.

If you are a student and you are playing the role of the class clown who is always disrupting the lesson, you are not the teacher's favorite and most likely not appreciated by the students. The reason that you are playing the class clown role doesn't matter,

"Never underestimate the power you have to take your life in a new direction."

— Germany Kent

how you act today does. You have the ability to change your student role from clown to teacher's pet, or anything in between.

The trick is to evaluate which student role you are playing and decide which one you would like to play. Then you decide what behavior you have to change, behave in a new way every day, and keep it up until you change from behavior to habit, and you have changed your role.

If you have the role of neighbor, you can choose to play the role of busybody or the role of friend. If you are a spouse, you can play that role as a loving and supportive partner, or you can play it as an abuser. It is up to you. If you are a parent, you decide if you play that role through love or through anger and control.

The whole point is that you are responsible for determining how you are playing your roles in life and to change how you are playing those roles when you know a change is needed.

As always, you are in control.

Scripture for Thought

Be strong and courageous. Do not be afraid or terrified because of them, for the Lord your God goes with you; he will never leave you nor forsake you.

Deuteronomy 31:6

Add a scripture or quote of your own that will help you relate to this week's topic.

_____

_____

CHAPTER 14

Win Well, Lose Well

Everyone likes to play the winner role, and most of us work hard at winning most of the time. Winning makes us feel good and often earns us lots of positive attention, and this improves our self-esteem and self-confidence. Being a winner also encourages us to try more challenging goals throughout our life.

So; we all agree that the winner role is great, but how do you handle playing the role of a loser when that happens? Many people take losing as a failure, and by seeing themselves as a failure, they can become depressed and start to lose their self-esteem and self-confidence.

> *You should strive*
> *to be good*
> *at both winning and losing,*
> *and you will become*
> *better at life from either experience.*

We all work hard at winning most of the time, in whatever we are doing. We put a lot of work and time into our activities because we want to win. At the same time, we must remember we are not the only ones working hard. All the people we are in competition with are also trying to win. So, when we do win, we need to play the role with humility because next time it may be one of them who wins.

If we keep a positive attitude, the experience of losing can be a way to teach us how to play that role with dignity. This may help us to look at why we lost and can teach us that what we tried did not work, but if we continue to be motivated and keep working on making improvements, we may be successful the next time.

Always play the role of a competitor with grace and dignity and you will grow as a person whether you win or lose. No matter which part of your life you are working on at any given time, you may win, and you may lose. The trick is to benefit from both as you enjoy every day.

Scripture for Thought

"I have the right to do anything," you say—but not everything is beneficial. "I have the right to do anything"—but I will not be mastered by anything.

1 Corinthians 6:12

Good judgment wins favor, but the way of the unfaithful leads to their destruction.

Proverbs 13:15

What good is it for someone to gain the whole world, and yet lose or forfeit their very self?

Luke 9:25

Each one should test their own actions. Then they can take pride in themselves alone, without comparing themselves to someone else.

Galatians 6:4

Add a scripture or quote of your own that will help you relate to this week's topic.

_____

_____

CHAPTER 15

The Little Boy
and the Old Man

Most of us provides all the attention needed to support our children while they are growing up. If our young daughter drops her spoon we pick it up for her or allow her time to pick it up, so she feels good about herself.

Said the little boy, "Sometimes I drop my spoon."

Said the little old man, "I do that too."

The little boy whispered, "I wet my pants."

"I do that too." laughed the little old man.

Said the little boy, "I often cry."

The old man nodded, "So do I."

"But worst of all," said the boy, "it seems grownups don't pay attention to me."

And he felt the warmth of a wrinkled old hand. "I know what you mean," said the little old man.

From A Light in the Attic

If our young son wets his pants, we know he did not do it on purpose. Without wanting to embarrass him, we help him change his clothes and do not make a scene about it.

If our young children start to cry, we ask why and work very hard to understand what made them cry. We reassure our children that it is okay to cry, and those who love them will hold their hand until they feel better.

If our young child is looking lonely, we will sit with him and make sure he is included more with the family activities until he stops feeling like no one is paying attention to him.

Why is it, after being given all the support and attention that we need as children, we treat those who gave us that support with such abandon?

Why is it, that after being made to feel good when we were down, being picked up after when we dropped things and being helped to feel good after we might have embarrassed ourselves, we are not willing to return that same love and support when it is needed to those who gave it to us.

How do we treat our parents and grandparents as they seem to require more and more attention? Do we put ourselves in their place, and try to imagine how it feels to slowly lose the ability to do things they have done all their lives?

Let's remember to treat those who took care of us when we were children with respect and dignity, just as they did for us.

Scripture for Thought

There is a time for everything, and a season for every activity under the heavens.

Ecclesiastes 3:1

But if anyone does not provide for his own, and especially for those of his household, he has denied the faith and is worse than an unbeliever.

1 Timothy 5:8

Likewise, ye younger, submit yourselves unto the elder. Yea, all of you be subject one to another, and be clothed with humility: for God resisteth the proud, and giveth grace to the humble

1 Peter 5:5

Add a scripture or quote of your own that will help you relate to this week's topic.

_____

_____

CHAPTER 16

Love Your Role

In life, we all play a role in every situation we are a part of. Sometimes we choose which role we will play, and sometimes it is given to us. You are born into your role in your immediate family, and that is not a role you can choose to change. You have a specific birth order, gender, and family culture.

As you grow, you can choose to change some of your roles, and how you play all of them. If you are the oldest son in a family of four boys, you will always be the oldest son. What you can do is

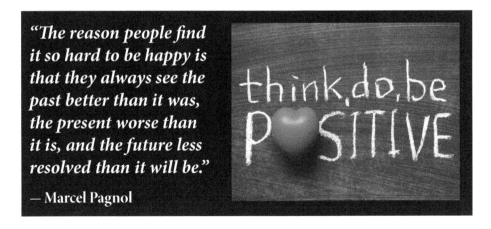

"The reason people find it so hard to be happy is that they always see the past better than it was, the present worse than it is, and the future less resolved than it will be."

— Marcel Pagnol

learn to love that role. You can treasure your time spent teaching your younger brothers and helping your parents with chores to keep the home running smoothly.

Let's say you are the mother of these four boys, and you are also an employee and a daughter to an aging mother. These three roles will keep you very busy, in addition to all the other roles you also play. If you can put your focus on the role you are playing at the moment, and learn to love that role, and appreciate the success you have when you play it, your life will be happy and fulfilled. If you resent the fact that you must play so many difficult roles, you will often find yourself disappointed and angry, and your level of success in those roles will go down, along with your happiness.

Most of us love many things and activities in our lives, such as the family dog, our favorite TV show, a certain sports team, or swimming. Why not look at our roles in the same way, as things we love to do and look forward to. The results may surprise you.

Scripture for Thought

Do everything in love.

1 Corinthians 16:14

Add a scripture or quote of your own that will help you relate to this week's topic.

_____

_____

CHAPTER 17

Time Management

D on't ever say you did not have enough time. You have exactly the same number of hours per day that were given to Helen Keller, Louis Pasteur, Michelangelo, Mother Teresa, Leonardo da Vinci, Thomas Jefferson, and Albert Einstein.

What did these people do that a lot of us don't?

The thing they did was do a good job in their role as a time manager. They made sure that what they saw as a priority, had as much time as it needed.

> *"Time is the most valuable coin in your life. You and you alone will determine how that coin will be spent. Be careful that you do not let other people spend it for you."*
>
> — Carl Sandburg

How many times have we said, "There just wasn't enough time to get it done; I'll finish it tomorrow."? We sometimes take on more than we are physically able to do in the time allotted, just to make someone else happy. That person could be your boss who you are trying to impress or your wife who you are trying to make happy. A lot of the time we genuinely start with a realistic day of work planned, and WE screw it up. What we need to learn is that we are the only ones who can play the role of time manager of our lives. Others can help us, but we are always in control.

When we are asked if we could do something more, a lot of us say yes, because we believe we can fit it in somehow and still get all our other work done. Not only do we end up not completing all of our work, but by rushing, the quality of all the work will suffer as well.

Most of us normally do not have a problem figuring out how much work we can do in an allotted time; our problem is sticking to the schedule we create.

We would be much better off if we were honest, and explained that it did not look like we had enough time today, but we will be happy to work on the task when we had some time and will finish it as soon as possible.

If others seem to do a better job playing their role in time management, we could just ask them how, or maybe just watch them and see what they are doing differently.

If we learn at an early age how to play the role of time manager of our own lives and to plan and manage our time daily, we will find we are much more productive each day and this skill will stay with us as we grow up and take on bigger and more complicated roles.

The one thing we all have in common is the amount of time in the day. The difference is how we manage that time.

Scripture for Thought

Let us not become weary in doing good, for at the proper time we will reap a harvest if we do not give up

Galatians 6:9

¹There is a time for everything, and season for every activity under heaven: ²a time to be borne and a time to die, a time to plant and a time to uproot, ³a time to kill and a time to heal, a time to tear down and ta time to build, ⁴a time to weep and a time to laugh, at time to mourn and a time to dance, ⁵a time to scatter stones and a time to gather them, a time to embrace and a time to refrain, ⁶a time to search and a time to give up, a time to keep and a time to throw away, ⁷a time to tear and a time to mend, a time to be silent and a time to speak, ⁸a time to love and a time to hate, a time for war and a time for peace. ⁹What does the worker gain from his toil? ¹⁰I have seen the burden God has laid on men. ¹¹He has made everything beautiful in its time. He has also set eternity in the hearts of men; yet they cannot fathom what God has done from beginning to end. ¹²I know that there is nothing better for men that to be happy and do good while they live. ¹³That everyone may eat and drink, and find satisfaction in all his toil— this is the gift of God.

Ecclesiastes 3:1-13

Add a scripture or quote of your own that will help you relate to this week's topic.

_____

_____

CHAPTER 18

Good When Convenient

Most adults in America are guilty of the behavior of being a good neighbor only when it is convenient. We care about our neighbors, and we want to help them, but we are not usually willing to sacrifice much to do this.

If my co-worker needs a ride home, I'm happy to provide it, as long as it doesn't inconvenience me. So often, we can be heard to say, sure, I'll help *if I can*. We brag about our good deeds, but should we be bragging about doing something that does not cause

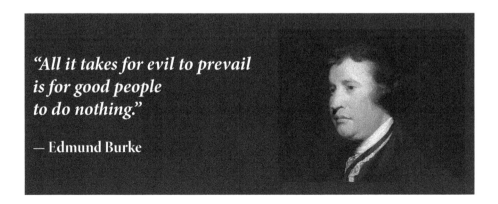

"*All it takes for evil to prevail is for good people to do nothing.*"

— Edmund Burke

us any difficulty? The ones who can brag are those who help when it is hard, and when it does inconvenience them.

This is a topic that we will all do well to ask ourselves what role we play in our community when it comes to helping our neighbor. Do we play the role of a helpful neighbor when we see a need, or do we claim to be that, but only play that role if it is convenient for us?

A good example of evil in our nation today is domestic violence. This horrible behavior is alive and well in many of our families today, and we all look at the sad stories and ask, why didn't someone stop this? Did no one know?

Someone always knows. They just do nothing because it is not convenient. Putting yourself in the position of Good Samaritan often comes with baggage. If you call the authorities on the neighbor who you know is abusing his wife, who will help her and her children when they take the husband to jail? Does that burden lie with the one who called the police? Is that person in a position to follow through with what comes next? Who will help you when the angry husband gets out of jail, and comes looking for the informant?

The role most of us play in this situation is that of burying our head in the sand. What we don't know, we can't do anything about, right? It's not my fault they suffered so; I was not aware of what was happening.

Another good example of us being a good human being, but only when it is convenient, is that of providing help to the disabled, or families of deployed service men and women.

If any American spent 10 minutes thinking about and researching, the lives of the disabled, or the families of those deployed away from home in the service of our nation, we could not honestly say there was nothing we could do.

We are all happy to give our $10 when the bucket comes around at work for most causes, and then we brag about it for a year. While that is a good thing to do, and it does make a difference in most cases, that is a drop in the bucket to what we could actually do if we were willing to be inconvenienced a little.

If you are reading this book, and you stopped for ten minutes, you could probably write a list of at least ten ways you could help someone in one of these groups. Why don't you just start writing, and then choose one item from your list, and do it? The rewards you will experience will be equal to those of the one you help, may be greater.

What role do you want to play as a member of the American community?

Scripture for Thought

Now all has been heard; here is the conclusion of the matter: Fear God and keep his commandments, for this is the duty of all mankind.

Ecclesiastes 12:13

Bear one another's burdens, and so fulfill the law of Christ.

Galatians 6:2

And let us not grow weary of doing good, for in due season we will reap, if we do not give up.

Galatians 6:9

Let each of you look not only to his own interest, but also to the interests of others.

Philippians 2:4

Open your mouth for the mute, for the rights of all who are destitute. Open your mouth, judge righteously, defend the rights of the poor and needy.

Proverbs 31:8-9

Add a scripture or quote of your own that will help you relate to this week's topic.

_____

_____

CHAPTER 19

Keeping Your Word

When entering into any agreement, consider what your role will be, and how you will play it. When we make an agreement with someone, we both have reasons for entering into the deal. We both have expectations, and we both have a role to play. This is all established at the beginning, and then we choose how we play the role we agreed to.

Giving our word is very important when we do it, and the agreement is made for and by both people involved. Consider that if you do not play your role in the agreement with honor you

Every time you make an agreement with another person, and give them your word to keep that agreement, you are putting your relationship with that person at risk.

DELIVER ON YOUR PROMISES

are telling the other person that the promise you made, as well as their relationship, is no longer important to you.

Many of us make a deal wanting instant gratification, and we do not think past our satisfaction at the moment. Our role right then is a problem solver and not a protector of our word. The cost of solving our problem and getting what we want at the time may, in the end, be more than we can afford to pay.

Think ahead. When you make a promise, make sure you understand your role in the agreement. Realize that if you break your promise, you will let both the other person and yourself down. Consider why you gave your word in the first place and don't let anything stop you from keeping it.

Your word may have been very important to the other person, and if you break it they may feel let down by you, especially after they put so much trust in you, and they made sure they were living up to their end of the promise.

It always takes more time and energy to go back and repair the damage you caused when you broke your word than it would have taken to keep your bargain in the first place.

Scripture for Thought

Do not be deceived: God cannot be mocked. A man reaps what he sows.

Galatians 6:7

For this is what the Lord, the God of Israel, says: "The jar of flour will not be used up and the jug of oil will not run dry until the day the Lord give rain of the land"15 She went away and did as Elijah had told her. So there was food every day for Elijah and for the woman and her family. 16 For the jar of flour was not used up and the jug of oil did not run dry, in keeping with the work of the Lord spoken by Elijah.

1 Kings 17:14 – 16

Add a scripture or quote of your own that will help you relate to this week's topic.

_____

_____

CHAPTER 20

Better Than Yesterday

W hen you look at how far you have come toward reaching your goals, the first thing you need to look at is what role you are playing in that. Are you in charge of the little goals you set for yourself each day, and of doing what has to be done to reach those goals? Others can help you and give you ideas and solutions to small problems along the way, but it is up to you to make sure that you end each day closer to your goal than the day before.

Make yourself better than yesterday, every day!

Don't work on being better than anyone else. Work on being better than you were yesterday. It's not enough to just settle for being OK at life. Every day should be a learning and growing experience, and you should use that experience to become a better you every day.

Look at your neighbor with interest, and maybe get some ideas, but pay no attention to how you compare to her. How you compare with the girl next door, or how she got to be better or worse than you is really not relevant to your daily goal. That goal is what you focus on, and that is what will get you to where you want to be.

When you make a mistake, take responsibility for it. Even if someone else talked you into doing something, and you failed, you still must look for your role in the failure. What could you have done differently? Look at it, learn from it, and move on. Blaming someone else will not help anyone, so don't waste your time.

Learning how not to do something is what stops you from making the same mistake twice.

If the girl next door appears to be getting ahead faster, be glad for her, and try to learn from her today. Tomorrow she may fall on her face from going too fast and have to start over. You just keep going at your own pace.

When you save money for a certain item, like a new car, the longer you save, the more fun it becomes. At first, the small amount you put away each week seems too little to make a difference. But if you stick with it, after a few months, you realize that it does make a difference, and you are starting to get close to your goal.

You can look at your life goals in the same way. What you put into the bank of your life each day, adds up just like the money, and before you know it you have a life to be proud of, and you have accomplished many of your dreams. Isn't that what it is all about?

Scripture for Thought

Do everything without grumbling or arguing, so that you may become blameless and pure, children of God without fault in a warped and crooked generation. Then you will shine among them like stars in the sky as you hold firmly to the word of life.

Philippians 2:14-16

But he gives more grace. Therefore it says, God opposes the proud, but gives grace to the humble.

James 4:6

If I must boast, I will boast for the things that show my weakness.

2 Corinthians 11:30

Add a scripture or quote of your own that will help you relate to this week's topic.

_____

_____

Make Your Role Work for You

W e each play many roles every day of our life. Some days the roles are easy to play, and you give very little thought to them. You move from the role of wife to mother, to driver, to employee to … Well, you get the idea. It is never ending.

The thing that may help you to enjoy those roles and to make the most out of them is if you can play the roles creatively. You are going to drive the carpool to school, so why not throw on a funny hat and put on some fun music to go with it while you drive the

> *What is success? I think it is a mixture of having a flair for the thing that you are doing; knowing that it is not enough, that you have got to have hard work and a certain sense of purpose.*
>
> — Margaret Thatcher

kids to school? They will then go into school with smiles on their faces, and you will feel energized instead of drained as you head to your next role.

We are going to play our roles and do our work every day, so why not find ways to play the roles that make them more enjoyable for you, and more productive. The trick is to break your day down into your roles and deal with them one at a time.

If a role requires you to be very detailed and accurate with some work, make sure you are properly rested and prepared for that task. If your next role allows you some flexibility, find some fun music or something that will lighten the mood.

The point is to give some thought to how you are playing each role and make each one work for you.

Scripture for Thought

And over all these virtues put on love, which binds them all together in perfect unity.

Colossians 3:14

Add a scripture or quote of your own that will help you relate to this week's topic.

_____

_____

CHAPTER 22

Encourage Innovation

T here is a difference between telling someone to do a specific task and encouraging them to find the best way to do that task.

Even children do not like to be told what to do all the time. Instead of telling them exactly how to do something, show them what needs to be done, explain the guidelines, and then encourage them to find a way to do it. Then, acknowledge them when they are successful.

Resist telling people how something should be done. Instead, tell them what needs to be done. Then let them decide how to do it. They will often surprise you with their creative solutions.

Most people, when given a role to play in a certain task like to be left alone to decide how they will play that role. They like the challenge of figuring out how to do it, and then the great feeling of accomplishing it. They don't get the challenge or the accomplishment if they are told the details of how they must play the role.

J.P. Getty was quoted as saying, "Find the guy who is getting his job done, and still sitting down more than the rest of the crew. See what he is doing and copy it for the rest." This would not only make work smoother for the rest but would allow the company to increase production. Innovation is usually a win-win situation. Many people, both children, and adults are interested in playing their role well, whatever that role is at the time. If they are allowed, they will often become very creative and ingenious with new and better ways of playing it, and thus getting the job done.

A good strategy to use as a parent or a manager is to allow certain limited latitudes when assigning jobs. Giving people a little latitude in how things are done, and supporting them with what they need to be successful, will create a lot of pride and satisfaction.

Scripture for Thought

As water reflects the face, so one's life reflects the heart.

Colossians 3:14

Add a scripture or quote of your own that will help you relate to this week's topic.

_____

_____

CHAPTER 23

Perception

The cowboy poet Will Rogers once said: "I never met a man I didn't like." Does that mean he liked everyone he ran into? It probably does not. It could mean, however, that he took the time to see something that he did like in the ones he met, even if it was a tiny thing, it was something he could like, and thus he liked the person. He used his personal skills to control his perception of people.

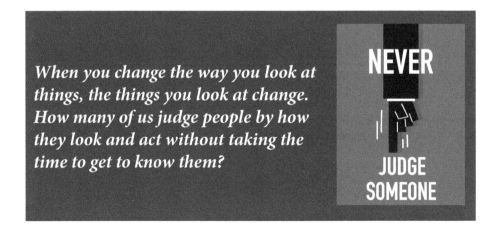

When you change the way you look at things, the things you look at change. How many of us judge people by how they look and act without taking the time to get to know them?

NEVER JUDGE SOMEONE

It is true, that if we can take the time, and change the way we look at things and people, what we look at and how we look at it would change.

If we learn the skill of finding something good in all situations, we will then be open to seeing everything around us more clearly and to the discovery of so much more in our lives. We will have people and opportunities in front of us that we never saw before because we were only looking for the problems and not the opportunities.

If the new girl starts work the week after her mother passed away, your perception of her will likely be one of a sad, keep to-herself kind of person. But, the woman who worked with her at her last job perceives her as a happy, life-of-the-party girl, who is always in a good mood. This is the same person, yet two individuals see her in two totally different lights. If we can all keep in mind that our perceptions are enhanced or hindered by unknown details, we would be better able to keep perceptions fluid and allow them to change as the situation changes. When the new girl starts to be more friendly a couple of months after she began her job, accept that as a good thing, and not as something to gossip about.

As adults, we must give ourselves as many different options in life as we can, and a way to do this is to look at our environment with an open mind and look for the beneficial factors in every situation as we form our perceptions. In all aspects of life, we have the choice to see the same reality with a positive perception, or with a negative perception. It is up to us to put the slant on things that can make our day what we want it to be.

I, for one, want mine to be pleasant.

Scripture for Thought

Do not conform to the pattern of this world, but be transformed by the renewing of your mind. Then you will be able to test and approve what God's will is—his good, pleasing and perfect will.

Romans 12:2

Do not judge so that you will not be judged. "For in the way you judge, you will be judged; and by your standard of measure, it will be measured to you. "Why do you look at the speck that is in your brother's eye, but do not notice the log that is in your own eye?

Matthew 7: 1-5

Add a scripture or quote of your own that will help you relate to this week's topic.

_____

_____

CHAPTER 24

Helping Hand

We all need help at times and it should not come with a price attached to it.

When we lend a hand, it is normally because someone needed it and we feel we are in a position to help. When we offer help to someone in need, there is no pay-back price on it. If there is a payback price, the payback will be you both have a good and honest friend for life.

The situation above is the best, and hopefully, it will be how you and your friends behave. The reality is often a different picture, and we don't always play the friend role the best way we

Lending a helping hand should be a joyful thing to do and should come from the heart.

could. Many times the friend role gets very complicated when it comes to providing help of any kind. We assume we are friends, so we don't lay out clear expectations about the agreement. This often leads to hard feelings and damaged friendships.

The safest way to play the friend role when it comes to giving or getting a helping hand is to make sure you repay the kindness if you are the one receiving the help, and that you have no expectations of being repaid if you are the one giving the help. If you can do that, you can most likely keep your friends.

Try to evaluate the situation clearly before you decide how you will participate in helping or being helped. Make sure that the need is great enough to risk the friendship over. Often it is. If the friendship is strong and you both play your roles out of love, your friendship should be able to weather the storm and stay strong.

Please remember there is no obligation to being someone's friend.

Scripture for Thought

When I said, "My foot is slipping," your unfailing love, Lord, support-ed me.

Psalm 94:18

⁶Then Peter said, "Silver or gold I do not have, but what I have I give you. In the name of Jesus Christ fo Nazareth, walk." ⁷Taking him by the right hand, he helped him up, and instantly the man's feet and ankles became strong.

Acts 3:6-7

³⁰*Simon's mother-in-law was in bed with a fever, and they told Jesus about her.* ³¹*So he went to herm took her and helped her up.*

The fever left her and she began to wait on them. ³²*That evening after sunset the people brought to Jesus all the sick and demon-possessed.* ³³*The whole town gathered at the door,* ³⁴*and Jesus healed many who had various diseases. He also drove out many demons. But he would not let the demons speak because they knew who he was.* ³⁵*Very early in the morning, while it was still dark, Jesus got up, left the house and went off to a solitary place, where he pryed.*

Mark 1:30-35

Add a scripture or quote of your own that will help you relate to this week's topic.

_____

_____

CHAPTER 25

Being Liked

The quote below will be familiar to many of you, and it will be understood by most. It refers to the age-old concept that you can't please everyone. No matter how you try, there will always be someone who doesn't like you.

Most of us want to be liked as we play all the various roles in our lives. We want to be liked by our family members, our co-workers, our neighbors, and of course, our friends. We will address the friend relationship here, but understand that the same thing applies in all of our relationships.

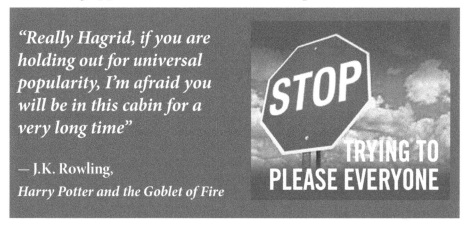

"Really Hagrid, if you are holding out for universal popularity, I'm afraid you will be in this cabin for a very long time"

— J.K. Rowling,
Harry Potter and the Goblet of Fire

STOP TRYING TO PLEASE EVERYONE

Playing the role of a friend. When it comes to considering how we play the role of friend and neighbor, we must consider how much energy we will put into playing a role in a way that will get more people to like us. This is a skill that it will be very worthwhile for most of us to build upon.

We can play the role of a friend with a goal of being liked, or we can play the role of a friend with a goal of being a good friend. This is the same role, but the two ways to play it have very different requirements, and very different results.

When we play our friend role with the goal of being liked, we are focusing on ourselves and trying to gain something from the relationship. This type of focus most often ends poorly.

When we play our friend role with the goal of being a good friend, we are focusing on others, and how we can play our role in a way that makes them feel like they have a worthwhile friend. This type of focus usually ends well. Nothing makes someone like a person more than when they perceive the other person as being there for them.

When you walk into a group of your friends, put your focus on them, and not on yourself. They will not even notice that you have a coffee stain on your shirt if you first greet them with a warm smile and a pleasant comment. If you do that with as many of the friends in the room as you can, you will feel welcome and comfortable, and so will they.

If you want to be liked by others, play your friend role with behaviors that show that you like and appreciate others. Remember another old saying, "If you want a friend, be a friend." It works.

Scripture for Thought

Finally, brothers and sisters, whatever is true, whatever is noble, whatever is right, whatever is pure, whatever is lovely, whatever is admirable—if anything is excellent or praiseworthy—think about such things.

Philippians 4:8

Do not be unequally yoked with unbelievers. For what partnership has righteousness with lawlessness? Or what fellowship has light with darkness? What accord has Christ with Belial? Or what portion does a believer share with and unbeliever?

2 Corinthians 6:14-15

Therefore, having put away falsehood, let each one of you speak the truth with his neighbor, for we are members one of another.

Ephesians 4:25

Add a scripture or quote of your own that will help you relate to this week's topic.

_____

_____

CHAPTER 26

Play Your Role Like a Rock

Each of us can think of a person we have known in our life who we would label as a rock. This is someone who we trust, and who we depend on to always behave in the same way. These are the people who have long funeral processions because they will be missed by many.

The special thing about these people, these *rocks*, is that they behave the same almost all the time and in all the roles they play. No matter what role they are playing, they can be expected to do what they always do. This role of *rock* doesn't happen overnight.

It is not the beauty of a building you should look at; its the construction of the foundation that will stand the test of time.

— David Allan Coe

It takes a conscious decision to behave in a certain way, such as to always be polite. If you make that decision and stick with it until it is a habit, before long, you will be known as that very polite person. No matter what role you are playing at the moment, you will play it, and others will expect you to play it with manners.

Once you build one habit, try some others: kindness, fairness, compassion, understanding, empathy, etc. etc. Every habit you add will make you more of a *rock* in all your roles.

Scripture for Thought

Truly he is my rock and my salvation; he is my fortress, I will never be shaken.

Psalm 62:2

Add a scripture or quote of your own that will help you relate to this week's topic.

_____

_____

CHAPTER 27

Follower or Leader

Whether you play the role of follower or leader is a choice you make many times through your life. We make that choice in all the different roles we play in our lives: as a student in school, on the playground, as an employee, as a family member, as a community member, and in many other situations.

When you are in your early teens and begin to grow up, you make a choice about whether you will play the overall role of follower or leader in your life. This is sometimes a conscious choice, but for most it is subconscious, and your personality and your

"The best is he who calls men to the best. And those who heed the call are also blessed. But worthless who call not, heed not, but rest."

— Hesiod,
8th Century BC Greek poet

behaviors determine which role you will play. While most people don't have the skills early in life to evaluate this role, it is something you can look at throughout your life, and make changes as you wish.

If you are going to be a follower (and that is OK; most of us are followers), you must choose who you are going to follow. Do the people you choose to follow have the same goals, morals, ethics, and integrity that you have, or that you wish to have? Do they have the best interest of those following them in mind, or do these leaders have their agendas that do not consider those who are following them?

As followers, sometimes you will be held responsible for someone else's decisions. Is this going to be something that you are proud to be connected with or something that embarrasses or shames you? If you choose to play the following role those are important things you need to think about as you decide who you will follow.

If your choice is to play the role of a leader, how do you want to play that role?

Do you want to play the leader role in a manner that causes others to follow you because you have the same goals as they do? Do you want them to see you as someone who will make them successful, or maybe you want them to follow you because they see you as someone who has the skills to accomplish the task at hand?

As a leader, will you be a positive role model and influence those following you to understand and respect community values and teamwork?

Will you lead by example and follow the rules, show respect for authority, i.e., parents, teachers, police, and other leaders, and accept the consequences of your actions whether good or bad?

As you play the leader role or the follower role, pay close attention to how you play it. You need to think for yourself because if you choose to follow the wrong leader or if you are a negative leader yourself, your choices will directly affect you, as well as those around you.

Scripture for Thought

Finally, brothers and sisters, rejoice! Strive for full restoration, encourage one another, be of one mind, live in peace. And the God of love and peace will be with you.

2 Corinthians 13:11

"Woe to the shepherds who destroy and scatter the sheep of my pasture!" declares the Lord.

Jeremiah 23:1

For to this you have been called, because Christ also suffered for you, leaving you an example, so that you might follow in his steps.

1 Peter 2:21

Add a scripture or quote of your own that will help you relate to this week's topic.

_____

_____

CHAPTER 28

Cool Off

There are a lot of people divorced, in jail, or dead because they acted without thinking. If they had just stepped back and given the situation a break and thought about how they were playing their role in the relationship, that may have been enough to solve the problem.

How many times do you look at something you said yesterday and ask yourself, "Why was it so important that I had to say that right then?" Did you really stop to think about what you were saying or doing, and about the possible results that might come from it? Probably not.

Give yourself an hour to cool off before responding to someone or something that brings out strong negative emotions. If it involves something really important — give yourself overnight.

When you say or do things when you are angry or upset, you need to remember that you are probably not thinking rationally any time you play a role in anger. A great trick to learn would be to stop moving and close your mouth as soon as you notice the anger or hurt welling up inside of you. Realize that you need to take control of the way you are playing your relationship role at the moment. Stand still, close your mouth, count to 10, or to 100, or count until you feel the emotions calm. Then think. Then talk. Then act.

The ones you usually hurt the most are the ones closest to you. When you speak and act without thinking, you risk changing your role in the relationship. When you put others in a position of fear or hurt, you are taking on the role of bully. No relationship has room for the role of bully. Your partner or your children are often the ones affected by what you say or do when you are angry. Aren't these relationships worth a few moments of cool down time? You will think they were if you lose them.

Remember the first action to take when you begin to play any role in anger is to stop and cool off.

Scripture for Thought

Those who guard their lips preserve their lives, but those who speak rashly will come to ruin.

Proverbs 13:3

Add a scripture or quote of your own that will help you relate to this week's topic.

CHAPTER 29

Happiness

T he old saying, "Money can't buy happiness" was true when
it was first said, and is still true today.

Money can buy possessions, and having possessions
can bring you instant gratification, and will make you *feel* happy,
and play a happy role for a little while. With possessions, the
happy role is easy to play at first. Who doesn't like to have a new

> *True happiness is not based on possessions, power, or prestige, but on how you manage your life and your relationships. Possessions get old and fall apart. Power comes and goes; it never lasts. Prestige is dependent upon others' opinions. True happiness costs nothing to give or receive, does not get old, will last forever, and does not require the opinion of others.*

toy? The problems come when the new starts to wear off, so we go buy another, bigger and better toy to replace it. We soon realize that the happy role possessions put us in are very short lived.

What about the power-driven happy role? Most of us know someone who thinks his happiness comes from being the boss and having control or power over others.

What we see him soon learn is that with power comes a lot of responsibility, others generally start to want things from you, have expectations for your behavior and your time, and your every move is judged. Consequently, as the power role increases, the happy role decreases.

From the role of possessions and power often comes prestige. People are quick to show respect and honor to someone playing the role of success. This prestige at first leads to the happy role for the one being honored. Your old friends are suddenly much more attentive and have a lot more time for you. New friends are at your doorstep, waiting to slip in and share the glory. Opportunities are awesome and everywhere!

Then, just as with possessions and power, prestige is often short-lived and/or an unpleasant role to play. The expectations are high, and the risk of losing it all is constant and demanding. It only takes one mistake to bring it all crashing down.

It's hard to play a sincere happy role, when under such pressure. Before long, the happy role is only a role being played for the benefit of others. The internal happiness that leads to a happy dance is gone, replaced by a false smile to go with false happiness.

True happiness is not based on possessions, power, or prestige, but on how you live your life.

True happiness is not based on possessions, power, or prestige, but on how you live your life.

Scripture for Thought

For this very reason, make every effort to add to your faith goodness; and to goodness, knowledge; and to knowledge, self-control; and to self-control, perseverance; and to perseverance, godliness; and to godliness, mutual affection; and to mutual affection, love.

2 Peter 1:5-7

I perceived that there is nothing better for them than to be joyful and to do good as long as they live.

Ecclesiastes 3:12

A glad heart makes a cheerful face, but by sorrow of heart the spirit is crushed.

Proverbs 15:13

Until now you have asked nothing in my name. Ask, and you will receive, that your joy may be full.

John 16:24

Add a scripture or quote of your own that will help you relate to this week's topic.

_____

_____

CHAPTER 30

Teach Our Children

How many of us really accept responsibility for our actions as parents when our children behave in unacceptable ways?

When our children's actions are inappropriate, do we ever look back at our parenting and acknowledge that they are doing what they watched us do? It's more likely that we, like so many others, blame the children and say, "We taught them right from wrong, they should have known better."

If we teach our children by example, then we have only ourselves to blame or to take credit for what they become!

As we think about the *role we play* as parents in our children's lives, what comes to mind?

If we believe that as parents, we are responsible for the actions of our children; then that must include both good and bad actions. Whatever degree of credit we decide we can take for their good behaviors and successes, we must take the same degree of credit for their bad behaviors and failures.

The *role we play* as parents does not change to suit us. It is probably the most important role we play in our entire life. We are not just molding the next generation; we are molding all the future generations. How we play this role matters.

When we think about this very important role, we all look at it through our own eyes. Some say, "I want my children to have more than I did while I was growing up." or, "I don't want them to be treated the way I was treated."

Those are both common thoughts by parents, and many of us have had similar ones. There are many others we can all think of because the role of a parent is one that causes everyone to reflect on their actions, as well as the actions of their parents and care-givers during their childhood.

The question to ask yourself as you are thinking about whether or not you are teaching your children to be responsible for their actions is: How would my children describe my role as their parent?

Would they say you set a good example for them to follow, or would they say they don't know what role you are trying to play, they just know they will play it different when it is their turn? It is in your power to change this at any stage of life. Live so that your children say they will play their role as a parent just like their parents did.

We are, in most cases as parents, legally and morally responsible for the actions of our children until they are legal adults.

It seems we are always ready to take credit when our children do well, as they become honor students, basketball stars, president of the student body, or have any number of positive accomplishments. When someone tells us that we should be proud because we have done a great job with our child, we say yes we are. His father and I are really proud!

We do not acknowledge that we had nothing to do with it. It's his accomplishment. We just provided the needed tools and taught him right from wrong.

When a child gets into trouble, the same person comes and tells you to watch your child better. It's then you say, "It's not our fault, we taught him right from wrong. He should have known better." This is where many of us make it all the children's fault and do not take responsibility because it will make us look bad.

The role of the parent begins at the child's birth and ends officially when the child turns 18. In reality, this role never ends. Our children look to our example at every stage of life. Even though legally, we are no longer responsible for them, morally we have an ongoing responsibility to provide an example of the right way to behave at every stage of life. We also hold the responsibility to not provide a bad example at any time. Your children never stop watching what you do. You can never let down your guard about how you are playing this very important role.

Scripture for Thought

Those whom I love I rebuke and discipline. So be earnest and repent.

Revelation 3:19

"Young and old alike, teacher as well as student, cast lots for their duties.

Chronicles 25:8

"Start children off on the way they should go, and even when they are old they will not turn from it.

Proverbs 22:6

"The student is not above the teacher, but everyone who is fully trained will be like their teacher."

Lake 6:40

Add a scripture or quote of your own that will help you relate to this week's topic.

_____

_____

CHAPTER 31

Teach Children About Roles

T he concept of a child playing a role is not something typi-
cally talked about, but it is what happens. When a four-
year-old is a little sister, she chooses how she plays that
role. Is she kind, and does she try to learn from her siblings, or
does she treat them bad, and refuse to do what they ask her to do?

We have all seen both types of little sisters, and how they get
to be the way they are is usually a mystery. The trick though is
to help them to understand that they have a lot of different roles
in life, sister, daughter, granddaughter, cousin, neighbor, friend,

Parents are the ultimate role models for children. Every word, movement and action has an effect. No other person or outside force has a greater influence on a child than the parent.

— Bob Keeshan

student, etc. If you can get them to think about that concept, and talk about all of their roles, they will be much closer to learning how to play those roles to everyone's benefit.

Take a specific behavior, maybe greeting people for the first time that day. Ask the child how she says hello to her mommy and daddy in the morning. There is a good chance that it is with some words, a hug or a kiss and a smile. Now ask how she says hello to her teacher at her daycare. She will probably say with words, a smile, and maybe a hug, but not likely a kiss. Now ask how she greets the waitress she sees in the restaurant. She will know that she uses only words and a smile to greet a stranger. She has just told you how she plays her social role.

This may seem complicated if you take it too far. The message to give to the child is that she plays a lot of different roles in her life, and she can play them well or poorly; it is up to her. She can be a sweet daughter who picks up her toys, or she can be a naughty daughter who throws her toys across the room. She makes those decisions. Your job is to teach her that her job is to make good decisions and play her roles well.

Scripture for Thought

No discipline seems pleasant at the time, but painful. Later on, however, it produces a harvest of righteousness and peace for those who have been trained by it.

Revelation 3:19

Add a scripture or quote of your own that will help you relate to this week's topic.

CHAPTER 32

Is it Working?

Why is it that many of us are so stubborn we will keep working on something the same way until it frustrates us so much we tear it up and end up throwing it away? It would be different if by continuing to work on it, we were making even a little progress now and then.

One insanity definition: doing the same thing over and over and over and expecting different results.

Sometimes we should put away what we are doing for a little while and come back to it later. Or better yet put away our stubborn, independent role and ask someone else to look at it and tell us if they can see another way.

"If you keep doing what you've always done, you'll keep getting what you've always got."

There is a lot to be said for the friendship role that lets us talk to others about something that is giving us trouble. But instead, many times we prefer the arrogant ego role and insist that we can figure out whatever it is by ourselves.

There is an old saying, *"you don't know what you don't know."* You find out what you don't know by first admitting to yourself you don't know it all, then go and find someone with knowledge of what you are working on and ask them. The key is to then listen! Make a change from the ego-filled problem-solver role to the open-minded, flexible problem solver role.

This concept applies to relationships the same as it does to projects. If you keep using the same strategy to try to fix a problem with a friend or coworker, you will likely never resolve the issue.

Again, you must look at the role you are playing in the relationship. If it is a friend, and you play the dominant role and always make the decisions and set the rules for your activities, maybe you could try to change to the role of an equal friend. This is something you can do by yourself, just start to view you and this friend as equal. Ask opinions and start to share the decision making. You will very likely start to see an improved relationship. No matter what the issue is, one good way to start to solve it is to stop doing the same thing and look at how you are playing your role. Then find a way to change that, and you will change the relationship.

Whatever you are struggling with, stop thinking that what you have been unsuccessfully doing to fix it will magically start to work. Instead, start thinking about how you can make changes to what you are doing, and how you are doing it, and new strategies

Will come to you. Keep making changes until you find the one that does the trick.

Scripture for Thought

So is my word that goes out from my mouth: It will not return to me empty, but will accomplish what I desire and achieve the purpose for which I sent it.

Isaiah 55:11

Add a scripture or quote of your own that will help you relate to this week's topic.

_____

_____

CHAPTER 33

Patient or Enabling

If we play our parent role with patience toward another person (partner, friend, or child) who is inappropriate or pushing the boundaries, hoping they will change their behavior, are we being Patient or an Enabler?

I know having patience is a good thing and I like it when others are patient with me.

> *"Educate your children to self-control, to the habit of holding passion and prejudice and evil tendencies subject to an upright and reasoning will, and you have done much to abolish misery from their future and crimes from society."*
>
> — Benjamin Franklin

Do the others (partner, friends, or child) understand I am being patient or do they think I am ignoring (enabling) their behavior and they are getting away with something? Do we as parents and adults understand when our patience turns to enabling?

When do we say, I have been patient long enough and what you are doing has to stop? If we can't do that, we then we are playing the role of an enabler.

Most parents, employers or supervisors want only the best for those that are still growing and willing to learn. We play our role with patience when we deal with young children, new employees, or anyone exposed to a new environment.

With our children, we are patient because they have so much to learn, but after we have explained the same thing to them more than once and they seem to be ignoring us, and we do nothing about it, it is then that we become an enabler.

The same with new employees, we are patient with them while they are learning a new job or skill, but after a while, if they don't seem to be learning and we don't do something about it, we then become an enabler. The skill is figuring out when we move from being patient to an enabler in the different life roles we play. The rules are not the same.

It is easier as an employer because you will have a written policy of training and job performance. If the employee does not follow the policy, he is given warnings, and if they do not motivate the employee, he is let go.

When working with our own children, we parents seem to have a hard time figuring that out how to play this role. If we had been consistent in our approach, from an early age, we may not become an enabler as they grow. Most of the time we wait way too long before we decide to look at how we are playing our role and decide to do something about it. By then our children have been enabled for so long that they resist any kind of behavior change.

One key to finding the balancing point is to be consistent in our parenting and to set boundaries as to allowable behavior.

Life could, would, and should, be so much easier.

Scripture for Thought

For the Spirit God gave us does not make us timid, but gives us power, love and self-discipline.

2 Timothy 1:7

[29]You warned them to return to your law. But they became arrogant and disobeyed your commands, They sinned against your ordinances, by which a man will live if he obeys them. Stubbornly they turned their backs on you, became stiff-necked and refused to listen. [30]For many years you were patient with them. By your Spirit you admonished them through your prophets, yet they no attention, so your handed them over to the neighboring peoples. [31]But in your great mercy you did not put an end to them or abandon them, for you are a gracious and merciful God.

Nehemiah 9:29-31

Add a scripture or quote of your own that will help you relate to this week's topic.

_____

_____

CHAPTER 34

Message or Messenger

Why is it we reject and at times get mad when some-one in authority over us our gives us advice, but we will listen to that same message from someone who doesn't have any responsibility for the outcome of our actions?

When we are young, we are open to advise from a messenger with no authority over us, such as our friend's parents, someone from church, or an older person we may know, when they give us the same message as our parents, yet we won't listen to our parents.

Think about this. Why is it that all the messengers we choose to listen to have little or no authority over us, and also no power

When someone is trying to give you advice and you are not willing to listen to it, is it the message you don't like or the messenger?

to enforce consequences? While in our society, they hold a higher position than we do, they have no real control over us, so when we listen to their message, it is our choice.

This same concept applies to us as adults. Our boss and the policeman are messengers with power over us, and the ability to enforce consequences, but our friends and neighbors do not. Why is it then, that we often question and complain about the messages that come from these authority figures, but not when the same information comes from our friends?

It seems as though we don't understand how we are playing our role as employee or citizen when we reject what we know is probably good advice. Are we playing our role in every situation in a way that is in our best interest?

We need to ask ourselves who the messenger is and what impact he has on us. If our role is under the authority of that person, why would we think we should play it in a way that defies that authority? No matter who is right, if someone else has authority over us they also have the power to enforce a consequence, such as firing or arresting us. Learn to play your life roles in a way that will serve your own best interests.

Scripture for Thought

Make every effort to live in peace with everyone and to be holy; without holiness no one will see the Lord.

Hebrews 12:14

[17]A wicked messenger falls into trouble, but a trustworthy envoy brings healing. [18]He who ignores discipline comes to poverty and shame, but

whoever heeds correction is honored. ¹⁹a longing fulfilled os sweet to the soul, but foos detest turning from evil.

Proverbs 13:17-19

²⁷I was the first to tell Zion, "Look, here they are!' I gave to Jerusa-lem a messenger of good tiding. ²⁸I look but there is no one --- no one among them to give counsel, no one to give answer when I ask then. ²⁹See, they are all false! Their deeds amount to nothing; their images are but eind and confusion.

Isaiah 41: 27-29

Add a scripture or quote of your own that will help you relate to this week's topic.

_____

_____

CHAPTER 35

How to Become a Bully

1. Pick on others smaller or weaker than you, who cannot defend themselves.

2. Pick on others not as smart as you and who cannot verbally defend themselves

3. Pick on others who have a physical disability and cannot defend themselves.

4. Pick on others who are a different race or religion and due to their beliefs will not fight back.

5. Pick on everyone you can find who will allow you to feel more powerful.

When you become good at these things and play this role well, you can call yourself a qualified Bully. You will be known by young and old as someone who will pick on anyone who won't fight back. Your role of Bully becomes more powerful as others lose their humility and self-respect.

People are not born bullies, but usually, learn how to play that role at an early age. No one teaches a child how to play the role of a bully; they learn from watching and from experience. Often they see the man in the house play the bully, and sometimes the batterer role with the women and children. Over time, as the boy watches this continue, why would he not take on that role as well? One of the expectations of children is that they learn to copy the behavior of their role models.

As parents, we need to be sensitive to the type of role models we are for our children when it comes to modeling how family members should treat each other. It is important for Dad to show by example that he will treat others, including those smaller or weaker than he is, with kindness and gentleness, and never abuse. It is just as important that Mom show by example, that she will not play the role of victim and accept herself or her children being treated with abuse, nor will she treat anyone else with abuse.

We cannot forget that behaviors are learned and that parents are the first teachers our children have.

Scripture for Thought

Be very careful, then, how you live—not as unwise but as wise, making the most of every opportunity, because the days are evil.

Ephesians 5:15-16

But as for the cowardly, the faithless, the detestable, as for murderers, the sexually immoral, sorcerers, idolaters, and all liars, their portion will be in the lake that burns with fire and sulfur, which is the second death."

Revelation 21:8

A new commandment I give to you, that you love one another: just as I have loved you, you also are to love one another. By this all people will know that you are my disciples, if you have love for one another."

John 13:34-35

Add a scripture or quote of your own that will help you relate to this week's topic.

_____

_____

CHAPTER 36

The Victim Role

We take on the role of victim for a lot of reasons. How we get that role is not usually up to us, but how we play it and how long we play it is up to us. The work of getting through the victim role is always difficult, and can sometimes be a very slow process, but if you focus on how you are playing that role, you will make it as easy as it can be.

Children are often the victim of different things out of their control. Many times, it will affect them and how others view them as they grow up. Often, within families or in small towns, a child who has been given the victim role will find it almost impossible to break out of, because everyone sees him that way. It's almost

"*The roles we play change with time and circumstances, and while we don't always have control over the roles we are placed in, we do have control over the way we play them.*"

— Mike Siver

as if the community without realizing it supports the victim role rather than helps the child work out of it and return to the role of a happy child.

Even though it may be difficult, no matter if you came into the victim role as a child, or as an adult, you can control how you play the role and how long you play it.

If you lost a loved one to death, and you were not ready for it, or you are a victim of a violent crime, you very easily settle into the victim role. Others feel sorry for you, and make excuses for less than perfect behavior, because of what you suffered. This is appropriate and helpful for a while, but if it continues long term, you go from being a victim to being helpless and a burden. The best thing we can do for anyone who has suffered a loss or has been the victim of a crime is to help them work through it and get on with their life.

Remember, grieving for something that has happened to you or a loved one is normal and needs to run its course, but that course must have an end.

The role of victim is a phase and not a lifestyle.

Scripture for Thought

The Lord will vindicate me; your love, Lord, endures forever— do not abandon the works of your hands.

Psalm 138:8

Add a scripture or quote of your own that will help you relate to this week's topic.

CHAPTER 37

Parent as a Role Model

As adults, when we play our role as parents, a lot of the time we do not appreciate the responsibility of role model. Oh, we understand what being a role model means, but do we, as parents really appreciate the importance of that role.

In the parent role, we hope our children will learn how to treat others, talk to others, respect authority, respect other races, religions, other classes of people, and generally have an open mind to things they do not understand. The best way to make sure this happens is to show them this behavior through our example. The children will follow whatever example we show them.

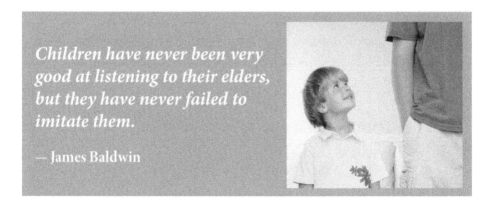

Children have never been very good at listening to their elders, but they have never failed to imitate them.

— James Baldwin

What our children also learn from our example is how to be a role model for younger children and for their children in the future. How we play our role as a parent, and the example we set with our behavior every day, will set the stage for the way our children play their own role in the future in all aspects of their lives.

Do your best to remember that children learn best by example, and whether they are your children or not, they will watch how you play your role as it relates to them, and will very likely try that role out at some point in the future. Make it a good one.

Scripture for Thought

May the Lord our God be with us as he was with our ancestors; may he never leave us nor forsake us.

1 Kings 8:57\

The Ten Commandments

1. Thou shalt have no other gods before me.

2. Thou shalt not make unto thee any graven image, or any likeness of any thing that is in heaven above, or that is in the earth beneath, or that is in the water under the earth: Thou shalt not bow down thyself to them, nor serve them: for I the LORD thy God am a jealous God, visiting the iniquity of the fathers upon the children unto the third and fourth generation of them that hate me; And shewing mercy unto thousands of them that love me, and keep my commandments.

3. Thou shalt not take the name of the LORD thy God in vain; for the LORD will not hold him guiltless that taketh his name in vain.

4. Remember the sabbath day, to keep it holy. Six days shalt thou labour, and do all thy work: But the seventh day is the sabbath of the LORD thy God: in it thou shalt not do any work, thou, nor thy son, nor thy daughter, thy manservant, nor thy maidservant, nor thy cattle, nor thy stranger that is within thy gates: For in six days the LORD made heaven and earth, the sea, and all that in them is, and rested the seventh day: wherefore the LORD blessed the sabbath day, and hallowed it.

5. Honour thy father and thy mother: that thy days may be long upon the land which the LORD thy God giveth thee.

6. Thou shalt not kill.

7. Thou shalt not commit adultery.

8. Thou shalt not steal.

9. Thou shalt not bear false witness against thy neighbour.

10. Thou shalt not covet thy neighbour's house, thou shalt not covet thy neighbour's wife, nor his manservant, nor his maidservant, nor his ox, nor his ass, nor any thing that is thy neighbour's.

Add a scripture or quote of your own that will help you relate to this week's topic.

_____

_____

CHAPTER 38

Leader as a Role Model

As leaders, we understand that it is our responsibility to influence those we lead, but often we lose sight of how important the way we play our leadership role is.

We know we must set a good example, but are we always aware that no matter where we are or what we are doing, we are a constant role model for those we lead.

When we are playing the role of leader in our workplace, our community, our church, a sports team, or one of many other leadership opportunities, how we play that role is critical.

"Setting an example is not the main means of influencing others; it is the only means."

— Albert Einstein

If we play our leadership role with integrity and behave in a way that sets the right example, we will find ourselves much more successful leaders.

If we set the example of spreading rumors and breaking the rules and procedures, we will find ourselves spending much of our time putting out fires.

As leaders, we set the standard for the way our followers will play their roles in the future. There is no question that if we want our followers to play their role well, we must set that example in the way we play our leadership role.

Whether we are leading a group of scientists in the search for a cure for cancer, or the children's softball team, we have the same responsibility to be a strong, positive role model at all times. It matters how we play the leader role. Play it well.

Scripture for Thought

Surely the Sovereign Lord does nothing without revealing his plan to his servants the prophets.

Amos 3:7

Add a scripture or quote of your own that will help you relate to this week's topic.

_____

_____

CHAPTER 39

Hatred

We have a choice in how we play our role in all of our relationships. We decide how much we let others control our emotions, feelings, and actions. If we take on the role of a hater, we give up a lot of energy because a lot is required to play that role, enough to make us tired at the end of the day.

As soon as we start to respond to another's negativity, we start to give that other person our power. If they know we are going to react each time they do what upsets us; they have control over

I will let no man drag me down so low as to hate him.

— Booker T. Washington

STOP HATE

us. So many of us do not understand that by playing our role in a relationship with dislike or hatred, we are letting someone or something outside of us control us.

We all have many relationships in our lives, and they are changing all the time, based on factors that are often out of our control. The one thing we do have control of in all of our relationships is how we play our role. It is up to us how much of ourselves we are willing to give to others.

When we take control of how we play our relationship roles, we also take control of our emotions and actions related to those relationships. This leads to us having control over our half of the relationship.

No matter what someone does, or how they act toward you, they do not have the power to change how you behave unless you give them that power. No one can make you hate.

Scripture for Thought

Hatred stirs up conflict, but love covers over all wrongs.

Proverbs 10:12

If anyone says, "I love God," and hates his brother, he is a liar; for he who does not love his brother whom he has seen cannot love God whom he has not seen.

1 John 4:20

Be angry and do not sin; do not let the sun go down on your anger.

Ephesians 4:26

Add a scripture or quote of your own that will help you relate to this week's topic.

_____

_____

CHAPTER 40

Building Bridges

O ur role in all of our relationships is to build and nur-
ture the relationship bridge. By definition, a relationship
requires two people, and both play a role in it. It is your
job to decide how you play your role and to play that role in a way
that will bring the results you are looking for.

Our lives are connected to the world through relationships.
They can be with family, spouses, bosses, friends, neighbors,
teachers, etc. There is very little we do in life that does not
involve a relationship. Within
these relationships, we have a
connection to the other person
that we often call a bridge. The
more important the relationship
is to us, the more care we take
in our role of building and
maintaining the bridge.

We build relationship bridges within our family, community, workplace, organizations, and on and on. If you think about the relationships that mean the most to you, you can probably see that you put a lot into building those bridges, and into maintaining them. In some instances, this results in your reputation. Whether good or bad, how you play your role will build your reputation.

An important concept to remember when looking at your relationships is how you play your role. Take the role of teacher/ student. As the student, you may think your role is to be on time, do what is asked by the teacher, and learn the material.

Do you ever look at what kind of bridges you build, and how you played your role in the relationship? There is a bridge between the teacher and the class, and between each individual student. The stronger the bridges are to each relationship, the more successful the entire situation will be for everyone. When you work on your part of the bridge, you encourage and support others in working on their parts.

The way you play your role as a student may very likely make a difference in the way the teacher and the other students play their roles, and in the outcome of the task at hand.

You have more power than you think.

Scripture for Thought

Speak up and judge fairly; defend the rights of the poor and needy.

Proverbs 31:9

Add a scripture or quote of your own that will help you relate to this week's topic.

_____

_____

CHAPTER 41

Don't Burn Bridges

You play a role in each of your relationships. You can play those roles with maturity and responsibility, or you can play them carelessly and risk burning the bridges that connect them.

After you tell your boss off and quit your job in a moment of anger, do you later wish you could take it back?

You say something hurtful to a friend, and burn that bridge, do you later watch that person in other relationships and realize you destroyed a future great friendship.

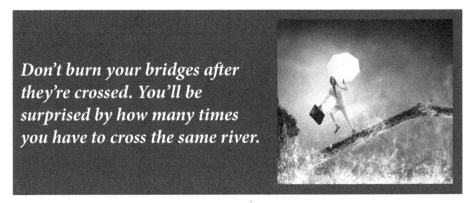

Don't burn your bridges after they're crossed. You'll be surprised by how many times you have to cross the same river.

We do not have future sight, and we will never know when we may need help, a job, or just friendship from someone on the other side of a bridge we burned in the past.

There are times in our lives when someone we thought was a friend said or did something that showed us he wasn't. Or someone worked for us, and we thought we could trust him, and it turns out he lied to us, or stole something from us. After we find out, we will say things such as, "Just wait till he needs something!" or, "I thought we were friends, why did he do that?" What happened is that he burned the bridge to your relationship.

What we need to be asking ourselves is, "Could I have done something in my role in this, to keep the bridge from being burned?" Often the answer is yes.

When we discover what the friend did, we could go to them and ask them about it, trying to resolve it before the bridge is completely burned. If we monitor our employees, we may see signs that theft is occurring, and discover that our employee has a severe and urgent need, and we are happy to help them find resources, and they keep their job, and we keep a good employee.

While we can't play the role of the other person, we can affect how they play their role by how we play ours. The bridge doesn't always have to burn.

We get offered a job but they are not paying what we think we are worth, and we tell them that, maybe with a little too much arrogance. They then give the job to someone else. Six months later we are still looking for a job, and will now take a job at almost any salary. We go back and tell them we have reconsidered, but they say, "No thanks."

The bridge was burned by the way we played our role as applicant. Rather than be arrogant, we could have thanked them, and said we had some other opportunities we were checking on, that paid more, but we appreciated the opportunity. Under these circumstances, we are not burning the bridge.

You are playing your role with maturity when you can disagree with someone, and resolve the issue without burning the bridge to the relationship.

Scripture for Thought

Blessed is the one who does not walk in step with the wicked or stand in the way that sinners take or sit in the company of mockers.

Psalm 1:1

Seldom set foot in your neighbor's house — too much of you, and they will hate you.

Proverbs 25:17

Add a scripture or quote of your own that will help you relate to this week's topic.

_____

_____

CHAPTER 42

How Far You Go

How far you go in life does depend on you being able to behave in the ways described in this quote by George Washington Carver. It also depends on you using these concepts to play all of the many roles you will play through your life.

If you play the role of parent and play it with these ideas leading you, what wonderful children you will have. If you play the role of a neighbor with these as your guides, you will never lack for a friend when you find yourself in need of a friendly face.

How far you go in life depends on your being tender with the young, compassionate with the aged, sympathetic with the striving and tolerant of the weak and strong. Because someday in your life you will have been all of these.

— George Washington Carver

In your life's vocational role, whether you be the employee or the employer, if you play that role always remembering these concepts, you will thrive and feel fulfilled at the end of each day, and at the end of your career.

It's a shame we often have to wait until we get older to understand the value of being able to give and receive empathy and sympathy.

Never forget where we came from and what it was like when we were young, and the times when we felt sad or helpless. Remember when we were weak and needed support when we were strong, and others put up with our ego. Remember how others put up with us when we became ambitious and sometimes unmanageable.

Understand that we will become aged one day and know how we would like to be treated.

As Mr. Carver so eloquently described, we all have been or will be in a position to receive empathy and or sympathy, so when we have an opportunity to play our life's role with compassion, we should do so.

Scripture for Thought

You are the light of the world. A town built on a hill cannot be hidden.

Matthew 5:14

Add a scripture or quote of your own that will help you relate to this week's topic.

_____

_____

CHAPTER 43

Who or What is Right
or Wrong?

Sometimes we make some people so important that we put them up on a pedestal, and we think everything they say or do is right. When these same people actually do something wrong; we might think they wouldn't do that, but if they did, then

We know in our heart what is right and what is wrong, but sometimes we are so influenced by someone that the black and white of right and wrong becomes gray. Do we decide what is right or wrong because of what our friends say, or are we strong enough to make up our own minds? Do we get so caught up in who's right and who's wrong that we forget what's right and what's wrong. Wrong is wrong and it doesn't matter who does it.

they must have had a very good reason. We put so much faith in them that we take on the role of protector of their reputation, rather than admit they may not be perfect.

Wrong is wrong, no matter who does it. Everyone thinks their have a good reason.

Sometimes our mind tells us how to play a role in front of us, and we feel in our heart what is right or wrong. Then playing our role the right way is easy. But, sometimes we are so influenced by someone that the black and white of right and wrong becomes gray. Then we find ourselves playing our role in the wrong way.

Wrong is wrong, no matter who tells you it isn't. Listen to yourself and trust your judgment. No matter who did it, or who said that what they did was not wrong, if you know it is wrong, it is wrong, period.

Playing the role of an ethical person means it doesn't matter who says or does anything, you know what is right or wrong, and you will do what is right.

Scripture for Thought

Trust in the Lord with all your heart, and do not lean on your own understanding. In all your ways acknowledge him, and he will make straight your paths.

Proverbs 3:5-6

But now apart from the law the righteousness of God has been made known, to which the Law and the Prophets testify. This righteous-

ness is given through faith in Jesus Christ to all who believe. There is no difference between Jew and Gentile.

Romans 3:21-22

You therefore, beloved, knowing this beforehand, take care that you are not carried away with the error of lawless people and lose your own stability.

2 Peter 3:17

Add a scripture or quote of your own that will help you relate to this week's topic.

_____

_____

CHAPTER 44

Play Your Role Well

Y ou play many roles, and how well you play each one is
your decision each day. None of us is at our best all the
time, and you will naturally have good and bad days, but
if you make it a conscious effort to play each role the best you can
that day, it will make a difference.

Playing your employee role well will, of course, benefit you
and your family. The more attention you pay to the details of
what is expected of you, the more successful you will be in your

*How well you play
your role determines
everything.*

employee role and this most likely will result in more money and more job security. Playing this role poorly will possibly result in not having to play it anymore.

How well you play your role as a family member is also critical to your well-being. The role of a family member is a large category that you can look at with a general, overall review. Are you kind and understanding and do you pull your weight when it comes to the work and the money? Do you take some of the responsibility to maintain family relationships and communication? These are just a few of the areas you can look at to help you decide how well you are playing this role.

The family member role should then be broken down into the specific roles you play within the family. Are you a son or daughter, a parent, a grandchild or grandparent, a sister, brother, cousin, aunt, uncle, etc., etc. You must look at the roles you play, and how well you are playing each one.

This task of evaluating how well you play your life roles can be huge. One way to approach this is to think about it once, looking at each role separately, and take stock of where you are now, and where you would like to go. Then just keep this concept in your mind. When something goes well, look at how you played your role in it so you can remember to play it that way again. If things go poorly, do the same thing.

The key is to accept responsibility for how you play each role and the consequences that may bring, both good and bad.

Scripture for Thought

Blessed are those whose ways are blameless, who walk according to the law of the Lord.

Psalm 119:1

Add a scripture or quote of your own that will help you relate to this week's topic.

_____

_____

CHAPTER 45

Be Successful

Throughout our lives, most of what we do is possible because of our family and friends and what they contribute to our path to success.

At every stage of our lives, most of us depend on family to contribute something to our journey. It may be just a word of encouragement, but usually, it is much more. And what about our friends, they always come through right when we need them. There are some rare loners, who become successful totally by themselves, but most of us work together to help each other reach our goals.

When you become successful in life never forget that you did not do it by yourself.

When we were smaller and involved in sports, who made sure we got there every night after school. Playing on the little league team doesn't happen unless we have parents who are willing and able to sacrifice to get us there day after day.

We take it for granted that's what parents do. We never think about how they have organized their evening just to help make us successful.

When we are older and involved in a social clubs or social activities that take us out of the house or away from our family, how much support does our family give us in order for us to participate that we don't even think about?

When we put in extra time at work to earn a promotion, do we think about how many people help us or sacrifice their time for us to become successful? Often we don't think about the ones around us who offer advice and direction. We can get so caught up in ourselves that we may ignore and reject some very important information, along with that magical word — Thanks!

When we finally do become successful and feel proud of ourselves, we need to remember we could never have done it on our own.

We must make sure we show the integrity that comes with that success and remember and acknowledge those who helped and sacrificed to get us where we are.

Scripture for Thought

Whoever pursues righteousness and love finds life, prosperity and honor.

Proverbs 21:21

¹¹Now, my son, the Lord be with you, and may you have success and build the house of the Lord you God , as he said you would. ¹³Then you will have success if you are careful to observe the decrees and laws that the Lord gave Moses for Israel.

1 Chronicles 22:11&13

Add a scripture or quote of your own that will help you relate to this week's topic.

_____

_____

CHAPTER 46

Forced to Agree

Have you ever noticed how many of the people we know think we do not understand what they are talking about simply because we do not agree with them? For some reason, they do not give us credit for having the brains God gave us. They do not accept the fact that we do have a brain and really do understand what they are talking about, we just choose not to agree with them.

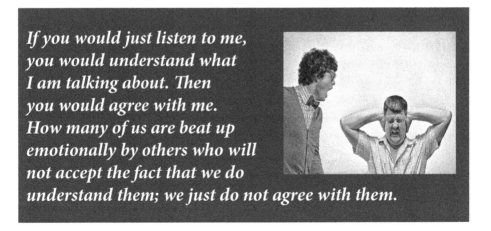

If you would just listen to me, you would understand what I am talking about. Then you would agree with me. How many of us are beat up emotionally by others who will not accept the fact that we do understand them; we just do not agree with them.

How often do we hear this type of communication? "Let me tell you again." "Let me re-phrase it, and you may understand it better!" "Will you listen to me this time?!"

Sometimes, it may even get to the point where we have to tell them we do not want to hear it anymore. We expect them to understand that we do hear them, and we do understand them, we just do not agree with them at this time, and most likely never will. Instead of this understanding, we often get an angry and defensive reaction, and continuous attempts to force us to listen until we do understand.

We all have things we are passionate about. We want others to join in that passion and support us, but not everyone will. That doesn't mean they are not listening. It may very well mean that they understand the point we are trying to make, they just don't think it is a good idea. It doesn't mean they don't like us, or that they think we are stupid or bad, they just don't like this particular idea. That is their right.

Ask yourself these questions: Do I want others to agree with me because I browbeat them until they say they agree, and it doesn't matter whether they agree or not? Or, do I want to know that they are listening to me and are not afraid to give me their honest opinion, even if they disagree with what I am saying?" Hopefully, you will settle on the second question.

Scripture for Thought

But you, man of God, flee from all this, and pursue righteousness, godliness, faith, love, endurance and gentleness.

1 Timothy 6:11

All Scripture breathed out by God and profitable for teaching, for reproof, for correction, and for training in righteousness.

1 Chronicles 22:11&13

Add a scripture or quote of your own that will help you relate to this week's topic.

_____

_____

CHAPTER 47

Protect Our Freedom

T his is one thing we are very passionate about. We wake up free each morning and have our military men and women to thank for that. Whether you have a desire to serve our nation in this way isn't important, but it is important that we all, each citizen and each resident of this great nation, show gratitude to those who are willing to serve. Without them, our future has no guarantees.

We live on the amazing Earth, full of different countries with their militaries, governments, religious and social beliefs, and

We are very proud to wake up each morning in America. God bless all our service men & women, past, present and future. You keep us safe and protect our way of life. We are grateful.

cultures. Just as each country on the Earth is different, so is each city in the United States of America. We have the right to live in any city we choose, and to practice our own beliefs and traditions. This is something we want to protect, and we are willing to support a strong military to do that.

If someone thinks maintaining our military is an option, what do you think would be the results of disbanding it? Possibly in some distant future, we as a world nation could develop the United Nations to the degree that they would serve as the world military, and we would all live in peace. We can pray for that, but we can't expect it anytime soon.

In the meantime, we must all play our role of US citizens and residents in a way that shows those who are defending us how much we appreciate their sacrifice and their efforts. We must support our veterans when they leave active service and attempt to return to their civilian lives. They are heroes and deserve to be treated as such. Please help our nation by showing them honor, and with the financial and medical support, they need. They deserve it.

Scripture for Thought

God is our refuge and strength, an ever-present help in trouble.

Psalm 46:1

Add a scripture or quote of your own that will help you relate to this week's topic.

_____

_____

CHAPTER 48

Don't Be Ashamed

W hy is it we are so unable to admit we are wrong when being wrong teaches us so much? If we are taught at an early age to look at the role we play in the things we do, then following our unsuccessful actions, we would look at what role we played and how we played it, and why we think it didn't work.

We should never be ashamed as we examine how we played our role and saw that we did what we thought would work and

> *A person should never be ashamed to say they have been wrong, that they made a mistake, or that they simply can't do something. Being perfect is not a goal any human being should have.*

this time we were not successful. With that knowledge, we can look at how we might play that role differently next time.

If we are not successful at something and we become ashamed, we may become afraid to keep trying new things. Once we get into that pattern of behavior, we no longer have adventure or enjoyment in our lives.

Those who are not afraid to try new things and embarrass themselves now and then will continue to grow and learn. Life for them will continue to be challenging and exciting. They will meet their unfulfilled challenges not with shame, but with determination.

A little humility can sometimes give us dignity and will allow us to keep our heads up. It instills in us, the motivation to study the ones who are a little more successful and to learn from others a better way to play our roles. We learn not only from others successes but from their mistakes as well.

Rather than be ashamed when you don't succeed, use failure as an opportunity to learn.

Scripture for Thought

Therefore confess your sins to each other and pray for each other so that you may be healed. The prayer of a righteous person is powerful and effective.

James 5:16

Add a scripture or quote of your own that will help you relate to this week's topic.

_____

_____

CHAPTER 49

Two Ears, One Mouth

This one is very simple in theory, but almost impossible in practice. We all play a communication role every day.

These roles vary greatly, and some require a focus on speaking, and some require a listening focus. Whatever role you are playing, make sure you keep in mind the two ears, one mouth ratio we all have. Even a school teacher, who must talk a lot all through the day, must listen more than she speaks.

How many of us play our communication role so heavy on the talking side, that we have talked ourselves into all kinds of trouble, some of it very serious, and if we would have just kept

We are born with two ears and one mouth. We should be listening twice as much as we talk!

our mouth shut and listened, everything would have been fine? We rarely get into much trouble while listening.

How many times when someone is trying to explain something or give us directions, do we interrupt while they are still talking by telling that person we understood them. Again, we should have been listening instead of talking. If we had to interrupt them, that meant that they were not finished with the instructions. We were just tired of listening and assumed we had heard enough.

One of the first skills taught in many leadership classes is the art of listening is much more important to a leader than the art of speaking. If you are training to be a dictator, this doesn't apply, but in the US, most leadership positions you will train for will require this skill. It is effective almost everywhere.

In one sentence, talk less, listen more. It works.

Scripture for Thought

Therefore confess your sins to each other and pray for each other so that you may be healed. The prayer of a righteous person is powerful and effective.

James 1:19

Making your ear attentive to wisdom and inclining your heart to understanding.,

Proverbs 2:2

If one gives an answer before he hears, it is his folly and shame.

Proverbs 18:13

Add a scripture or quote of your own that will help you relate to this week's topic.

_____

_____

CHAPTER 50

Guilty By Accusation

W hy do so many of us listen to, and repeat false accusations about others, rather than go straight to the person being talked about and just ask them about it? The most common response to this question is that it is just silly gossip. It's no big deal.

How many times have rumors caused you to form a negative opinion of someone? How many times have untrue rumors been spread about you or your family? Reputations, families,  *and lives have been destroyed simply because of false accusations. If you want to hurt someone, all you have to do is make an accusation. Accusation is one of the most powerful weapons used today in the daily power struggles in the American life.*

That is not how we feel when we are the ones being falsely accused.

This is where you must ask yourself, *"What role do I play?"* in the spreading of false accusations in my community or workplace? Am I the instigator, the one who makes up and spreads the false accusations? Am I the maintainer, the one who continues the rumor, and maybe makes it a little more interesting and thus more powerful? Maybe I am just a carrier, and I move the *harmless gossip* from one place to another. Or possibly I am the crusher, the one who crushes the false accusation, and stops the destruction of a piece of another's life.

If you ask yourself which role you are playing, you may be able to start being the crusher, and you may even be able to encourage others to join you in that positive role of being an agent of good, rather than of harm.

Scripture for Thought

[12]*A man who lacks judgment derides his neighbor, but a man of understanding holds his tongue.* [13]*A gossip betrays a confidence, but a trustworthy man keeps a secret.*

Proverbs 11: 12-13

You shall not spread a false report; you shall not join hands with a wicked man to be a malicious witness.

Exodus 23:1

Add a scripture or quote of your own that will help you relate to this week's topic.

_____

_____

CHAPTER 51

Your Future Roles

S tarting now, you are in control of your own future. You decide what you will do, where you will live, how you will entertain yourself, and everything else that will make up your life.

"How will I do this?" you ask. The answer is that you will control your life by controlling your roles and how you play them. If you pay attention to what roles you are playing, you can alter them to meet your needs at the moment, which will help you prepare your life for what you will need in the future.

> *At the end of the day, you're responsible for yourself and your actions and that's all you can control. So rather than be frustrated with what you can't control, try to fix the things you can.*
>
> — Kevin Garnett

If you are playing the role of student, you must stay focused on that role, and how you play it, so you make sure you have the career of your choice later. If you have the role of a renter, and hope for a home of your own, you must make sure you play the role of personal bookkeeper and saver, so when the time comes to buy a home, you are prepared.

Whatever your personal goals are, you must make sure you play your roles well today so you will meet your goals. When you do, be prepared to learn how to play the new roles that come with your success.

Scripture for Thought

Whoever pursues righteousness and love finds life, prosperity and honor.

Proverbs 21:21

Add a scripture or quote of your own that will help you relate to this week's topic.

_____

_____

CHAPTER 52

Your Name

When you were born, in most cases your parents took a lot of time picking your name. It is the one thing your parents could give you that will be with you all of your life. It is possible there is no one with your exact name, so it may be unique to just you. Your name was important to your parents and should be even more important to you because after they are gone you will still have something important they gave you. Treat it with care.

When we are young we never think about our actions and how they impact us. For example, one day you break a vase. The next day you throw a ball through the school window. You follow

Take personal responsibility for your daily endeavors. Act as if everything you do has your name on it.

> *"Make peace with your past. You are the sum of your experiences. Were it not for those experiences, you would not be the person you are today. I believe we are all born with the ability to turn our difficulties into opportunities. In owning all of it, I value the experiences, good and not-so-good, as blessings which ultimately created me, the person I am today. Without shame, I fully own my name, who I was, and who I am today."*
>
> — Patricia Bonelli

this with skipping school, hitting your sister, getting kicked out of the library for talking too loud, breaking a street light, etc.

If you continue these behaviors long enough, then the behaviors start to have a name, and unknown to you at the time, that name will be your name. You start to hear your parents and other adults saying, "Well, if anyone is going to do it, Charlie will. We just can't seem to slow him down."

At some point in the future, Charlie will start to realize there is a relationship between his behavior and his name, and he will see how people are referring to him and treating him. It's at this point that Charlie starts to consciously connect his behavior with his name. It's now he hears the principal tell his friend, Joe, "I better not see you pull a Charlie!"

As he goes on through life, Charlie should understand that people know about him who have never met him. If he continues to behave in the way described above, some will say, "Oh, you're Charlie. I heard about you." The tone in their voice will not be one of respect.

Charlie has the option to behave differently, and be the child who does the right thing instead of causing problems. If he always behaves in a good way, people will know about him and will say, "Oh, you're Charlie. I heard good things about you." The tone in their voice will be one of respect.

There are a lot of jobs and situations out there that will not even consider you unless you have a good reputation. If they don't know someone that can vouch for you, your chances are pretty slim. Even if they do have a reference, today most companies will do a complete background check on everyone. What we know but do not think about much is that right on the top of the background check is Your Name.

Another issue to consider is that when we get older, our children may start to have their own Your Name issues. They also may have had to live up to or live down your name.

With each generation, the one before sets the standard for the next one to live up to, or to live down. If you are Charlie's father, it is up to you to play that role in a way that if he continues to behave as described above, people will notice and say, "Boy, Charlie is nothing like his dad." Play your role so that this is what Charlie hears, and it is a motivation to help him change how he is playing his role of the son.

We all have the ability to behave in a way that will let us live up to our good family name, or to live down our bad family name. We also have the ability to create value in our Name.

So remember — If you do not respect your name, rest assured no-one else will!

Scripture for Thought

The name of the righteous is used in blessings, but the name of the wicked will rot.

Proverbs 10:7

And he must have a good reputation with those outside the church, so that he will not fall into reproach and the snare of the devil.

1 Timothy 3:7

A good name is to be more desired than great wealth, Favor is better than silver and gold.

Proverbs 22:1

"In view of this, I also do my best to maintain always a blameless conscience both before God and before men.

Acts 24:16

Add a scripture or quote of your own that will help you relate to this week's topic.

_____

_____

About the Authors

Mike Siver is a Master Addiction Counselor, Certified Domestic Violence Counselor and a Board Certified Biblical Counselor. Before retiring, he provided Anger Management, Domestic Violence, Substance Abuse counseling and assessments, and is a Chaplain for Forgotten Man Ministries. Currently is a co-facilitater for an IOP Subtance Abuse and life skills program based on his book "Why Did I Do That" for the local Veterains Administration.

He also facilitates a weekly program based on *What Role Do I Play* for young people Transitioning from jail back into the community.

April Siver was born in Michigan, the fourth of seven children. She received her public education in Southwest Michigan, her bachelor's degree at East Tennessee State University, and her master's degree at UNT in Denton, TX. She has worked in public education for 27 years. April has two daughters and four grandchildren, and resides in North Texas where she currently teaches high school. April also works as educational director for the nonprofit corporation, No Fences, Inc. where she uses her knowledge and skills to provide a helping hand to others through mentoring and tutoring.

April chose to co-author this book because she believes it to be a powerful tool for the No Fences program, as well as other individuals and organizations working to help people of all ages live the best life possible. It is her belief that no matter how hopeless things may appear, there is always a way to knock down any "FENCES" we may have in our way to turn things around. The trick is to keep trying.

Kirk Dusek grew up in Decatur, MI. He spent four years in the Navy (1994-1998) and was stationed in Virginia Beach, VA. He had one deployment on the *USS Georgy Washington*. After that, he worked for eight years as a Deputy Sheriff and was contracted to the US Army in Iraq doing Helicopter repair and maintenance.

Kirk has been married twice and has four children that he maintains a good relationship.

CPSIA information can be obtained
at www.ICGtesting.com
Printed in the USA
JSHW061034200523
41935JS00007B/129